TOMORROW'S
GARDEN

Design and Inspiration
for a New Age of
Sustainable Gardening

TOMORROW'S GARDEN

Text and Photographs by
Stephen Orr

RODALE

Rodale books may be purchased for business or promotional use or for special sales. For information, please write to: Special Markets Department, Rodale Inc., 733 Third Avenue, New York, NY 10017.

Printed in the United States of America
Rodale Inc. makes every effort to use acid-free ♾, recycled paper ♲.
Book design by Kara Plikaitis

Library of Congress Cataloging-in-Publication Data

Orr, Stephen
  Tomorrow's garden : design and inspiration for a new age of sustainable gardening / Stephen Orr.
     p.   cm.
  Includes index.
  ISBN 978–1–60529–468–1   hardcover
  1. Ecological landscape design.   2. Gardens—Design.   3. Urban gardens—United States.   4. Sustainable horticulture.   5. Sustainable agriculture.   I. Title.
  SB472.45.O77   2011
  712'.6—dc22   2010044385

Distributed to the trade by Macmillan

2   4   6   8   10   9   7   5   3   1   hardcover

We inspire and enable people to improve their lives and the world around them.
www.rodalebooks.com

For Chad

CONTENTS

Previous page: The notion of what makes a visually presentable front yard is steadily changing around the country. Dylan Robertson designed a garden in Austin, Texas, that avoids the usual roses and impatiens but still looks green and lush without wasting water. The emphatic silhouettes of blue agaves anchor wispier shapes of native lanceleaf coreopsis and grasses.

Black bugbane (*Actaea racemosa*)

INTRODUCTION

The Education of a Responsible Gardener

HOW DID YOU GET STARTED GARDENING? IT'S A QUESTION I'M ASKED QUITE OFTEN.
Like most gardeners, I refer to my childhood. Some of my earliest memories are of plants: feeding the roses with my dad, riding in the car to the nursery in the bright West Texas springtime, or admiring the bearded irises in our neighbor's front yard. Indoors, I trailed my mother as she watered the huge Boston ferns in the front window with tepid tea (for its acidity) and pinched back her collection of African violets on the living room étagère.

As a child, I was surrounded by the culture of growing things. My parents both came from agricultural families. My father grew up during the Depression on the dry, endlessly flat fields of a North Texas farm; my mother on humid coastal plains near the Gulf of Mexico. In Abilene, where I lived until college, Dad actively gardened our backyard for a number of years when we were kids. Even though the beds were small, he chose his varieties carefully and perhaps nostalgically from his youth: black-eyed peas, okra, peppers, flat green pole beans, and tomatoes—the flavorful varieties of vegetables that were, and still are, hard to find in many supermarkets.

Even though I usually tried hard to dodge anything resembling household chores, I was happy to spend hours in the summer tagging along with Dad as he puttered around the garden, planting seeds and helping him place old milk cartons over the tomatoes and peppers so that the seedlings would be sheltered from late spring frosts. I wonder now if he went to such effort for whatever actual produce the garden yielded, or if he had a broader plan to share part of his agricultural childhood with his children. Even in our dry climate, where the natural landscape was primarily prickly pear and mesquite, we didn't worry too much about conservation or issues like water usage. It didn't matter if our hybrid tea roses required a lot of chemical

Circumstances like shade and wildlife may keep the garden at my weekend lake house, *opposite*, minimal but even in the mossy environment surrounded by forests and lakes, *above and below*, I manage to grow enough flowers to provide new surprises each weekend. One May afternoon when the garden was at its peak, I picked this bunch of fritillaries, leucojum, hellebores, and grape hyacinths, *right*.

coddling, fertilizer, and fungicides to keep them in bloom. In fact, all the fussing and fretting might have made them more special. To be honest, I preferred our struggling bushes of 'Chicago Peace' to the wilder shrub roses along the back fence that seemed to thrive and bloom prolifically on nothing more than neglect.

During the 1970s, we had little concept of preserving resources on a personal level in our medium-size Texas town. Every lawn was bright green. Even though the city sponsored a drawing competition in my elementary school to see which student could design the best poster for the Lower Clear Fork of the Brazos Soil and Water Conservation District (giant sandstorms, the last vestiges of the dust bowl era, still billowed into town with some frequency), the contest inspired no ecological linkages in my mind; I just wanted to draw pretty pictures and win a blue ribbon. There was no preference for native varieties or consideration of plant suitability. We didn't care what harsh chemicals we must spray to achieve perfect flowers. Gardening for us was an act of forcibly bend-

ing nature to suit human will. It was considered highly admirable to thwart the natural cycle, to grow things in places where perhaps they didn't really want to be grown. Flower show prizes were given at the local fair for just this sort of horticulture.

But I loved flowers, and I still carry the plants I grew up with in my memory, a clear mental catalog of the flora of my old neighborhood, with each plant from the surrounding streets identified with its decades-old location. I knew every rose on the block and spent time going from bush to bush

like a honeybee to compare the different scents. I remember the wisteria on the corner and the pomegranate in the alley. The Faubuses, a retired couple across the street, had the best garden around, and I would follow Mr. Faubus like a shadow as he worked in his wide-brimmed hat and tan coveralls. Today, I vividly remember the old-fashioned plants he

taught me to appreciate: creeping phlox, hydrangeas, nandina, bridal-veil bush, lilacs, balloonflowers, bells of Ireland, balsam, santolina, and rosemary. Was there also a row of camellias on the side of the house? I like to think so. I saw magic in that garden that reminded me of places I read about only in books, like the Scottish manor house where the appearance of a ghost was preceded by the strong scent of heliotrope. I wouldn't see or smell heliotrope till many years later, but I can understand why the spectral lady selected it as her calling card. Soon enough, I grew up and

view of the Empire State Building on the other. But other days, it was a chore to be rescuing droopy dahlias in a heat wave at one in the morning. Even during drought years, I barely registered how much water I was wasting, where it came from, or where it was headed after it flowed down the drain, laced with sediment, vermiculite, and a liberal dose of bright blue fertilizer.

I had carried my childhood thoughts about gardening right up to that Manhattan rooftop. When I think of myself in the early 1990s, I was pretty naive ecologically. But then so were a lot of the people featured in the mainstream garden magazines that I followed so religiously. It was all about English gardening then, and Gertrude Jekyll was our mentor. Delphiniums and old roses were the order of the day. We were more likely to look across the Atlantic for inspiration than to anything that resembled an American gardening tradition. Our rooftop garden became my gardening education. During that period, I read books about horticulture or garden design and its history almost exclusively. My obsession led to a new career when I switched from magazine art direction to being a garden editor at *House & Garden* and then *Domino* magazine. Both jobs were fantastic. I traveled around the country (and sometimes overseas) documenting beautiful gardens with talented photographers, making lifelong friendships in the process. For a decade, my role was to look carefully at a garden and help the photographer see what was important for the readers. I was told by a more experienced colleague to read *The Education of a Gardener* by Russell Page. She said it would teach me everything I needed

became busy with school and the life of a teenager. My interest in gardening waned.

After several garden-free years in high school and university, I moved to New York City and found myself fortunate to have a rental apartment with a large rooftop space. It seemed to beg for a garden, since the bedroom opened out onto the roof through a sliding glass door and there was an outdoor hookup for a garden hose. I started small: a few herbs in cheap little window boxes and annuals in way-too-small terra-cotta pots that required constant watering. In fact, I thought little about how much irrigation my burgeoning container garden demanded as it grew both in number of pots and the size of the plants. The containers soon numbered in the hundreds, and it would take my partner, Chad, and me hours to water by hand. Sometimes this was our idea of heaven in the city, splashing around barefoot nine floors above the city streets with a choice between vistas of the Hudson River on one side of the rooftop and an unobstructed

Poisonous foxgloves easily fend for themselves. A new favorite hybrid, 'Pam's Choice', cuts a dramatically tall figure when seen against our dark house.

Why leave a yard full of daffodil varieties to wither during the week when you can cut them to appreciate the blooms back in the city? The coral-rimmed 'Audubon', below, is a standout.

to know about being a gardener. The 1962 book, by one of the 20th century's toniest garden designers, taught me a lot about the design of grand outdoor spaces and garden history. However, it told me nothing about gardens that sought to conserve (natural resources, labor, even money) rather than merely dazzle with the rigor of their perfection.

Not to knock Mr. Page; his gardens were amazingly beautiful. But as I stood at dawn in someone's walled potager in France or when I waited for the last rays of light in a large estate in California, the grandiosity of some of these private gardens began to unsettle me. Maybe it's my rather puritan Protestant upbringing or the practical voice of my mother in my head, but all the excesses started to weigh on me. Second and third homes or even spec houses sat empty of any furniture, but outside there was a full army of gardeners making the place look perfect in case the owner helicoptered in with prospective buyers. Around that time, I started to meet more gardeners and landscape designers who were making gardens with a conscience—sometimes even for the very wealthy. These properties weren't all about putting on a show; they were more concerned with fitting a garden into its proper setting, whether that happened to be the middle of a city or out in the country.

My own circumstances were changing as well. After 15 years, we had to give up the roof garden rental and move into a gardenless apartment, so we bought a cabin upstate with a small half-acre lot as a weekend getaway. The property is heavily wooded and, at any moment, surrounded by countless watchful eyes out in the forest waiting to see what tasty things I put in the ground. I have a deer problem. It has been an invaluable education in restrictions, especially after the rooftop garden where I could grow so many things (with enough fertilizer and water, that is). Now I have much more to consider before planting; faced with heavy, rocky soil, shade, animals, and hard winters, my gardening has become about paring down to essentials. Which ferns will grow where? Which bulbs will return more than just a year? Which plants are so poisonous that no hungry animal will touch them? On the other hand, some things are easy. There are the quiet joys of moss gar-

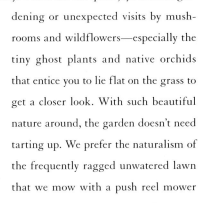

dening or unexpected visits by mushrooms and wildflowers—especially the tiny ghost plants and native orchids that entice you to lie flat on the grass to get a closer look. With such beautiful nature around, the garden doesn't need tarting up. We prefer the naturalism of the frequently ragged unwatered lawn that we mow with a push reel mower (such a nice sound, and good exercise). Foxgloves and helle-bores brighten the edges of the hemlock and beech forest. On country drives, I find myself gazing out of the window to admire the roadside plant groups for their effortless beauty: tall swords of verbascum mixed with feathery grasses and Oxford-blue chicory. It's a marvelous mixture of weed and wildflower, native and imported—and it's my favor-ite kind of garden these days.

It is this connection to nature in its biggest and smallest forms that now interests me most strongly while writing and thinking about gardening. Perhaps if you are holding this book in your hands, you feel the same. Maybe you are already striving to be a more respon-sible gardener. To that end, I propose a baseline of behav-ior. First, let's assume that all of us want to garden organi-cally. Everybody knows that such growing practices avoid the use of synthetic chemicals such as insecticides, fertiliz-ers, and fungicides. But a big-ger part of organic gardening comes down to a mind-set. Organic gardeners tend to allow for more imperfection in their gardens, whether it's a few bug-eaten leaves, a less-than-pristine lawn, or a year where the roses are given over to hungry thrips. You have to be a

After cutting down three diseased hemlock trees and gaining some welcome sunlight, I experimented with a tiny front-yard herb and vegetable patch, *above and opposite*. Shade-loving bulbs like the trout lily (*Erythronium* 'Pagoda'), *opposite top right*, thrive around the foundation of our 1930s lake cabin, *opposite bottom*.

little Zen and not too controlling about your plants when you take this approach, though it's a good exercise for the inner control freak in some of us—you know who you are.

It's all too easy to take a judgmental, hard-line approach that doesn't take into account this vast country that we garden in. I once received a letter from a reader at *House & Garden* who was angry that I did a story on growing English ivy as a houseplant. To her mind, I was promoting a rampant weed that would take over the woodlands. Checking the postmark, I could see that this reader lived in the Pacific North-west, where English ivy is indeed on the list of danger-ously invasive plants. Beside missing the fact that I was writing about houseplants, she didn't realize that in other, colder parts of the country (i.e., the Northeast), that particular ivy stays pretty much where you put it and doesn't enter natural areas. For all you plant pur-ists out there, be forewarned: You will encounter nonnative plants in this book. Worse yet, there are even some that may become invasive trouble-makers if put unthinkingly in the wrong place. The gar-deners who have planted imported species in the gardens

discussed here, however, are conscious of the potential dangers. They have done their research. You can't leave such questions to nurserymen and plant catalogs; in a large country with so many ecosystems and climates, we should all take responsibility for what we put in our yards. Unlike gardeners of the past, we have an amazing amount of online information at our fingertips. For starters, the gardening section of your USDA Cooperative Extension Web site has online information that is specific to your area, or you might be blessed with a responsible, well-staffed plant nursery nearby.

However native you choose to go, let's not forget that gardening is an unnatural act in many ways. When you consider many of the basic activities that constitute the act of gardening—importing plants (potentially from all over the world), irrigating with water (sometimes from distant or overtaxed sources), altering natural growth patterns, moving and regrading earth, imposing artificial barriers to keep out neighbors and animals, amending the natural components of the soil—it all can start to feel very antinature. In fact, the roots of the word *garden* derive from the act of enclosing a space, to guard it and separate our version of the cultivated from the wilder world. We humans love our gardens. They sustain us both spiritually and physically and can have an undeniably positive impact on the ecology of our local environment—but how do we make them responsibly? How do we create beautiful gardens without the waste?

The idea that we should grow gardens that are in tune with the natural world around us is not new. We've been through a series of movements over the past century: organics, biodynamics, sustainability, and permaculture. Several of these words are so much a part of our everyday lives now that they've almost lost their meaning; others remain unfamiliar to most gardeners. It doesn't help when marketers and adver-

When you have a limited number of plants that you can grow, you start to appreciate what arrives easily and naturally on its own. I may not be able to have roses, but dozens of varieties of lawn mushrooms and strange wildflowers like the ghost pipe, *opposite left,* make living in the middle of the woods worthwhile.

tisers pick up these terms and bandy them around to the point that we all forget their original definitions and intentions. Even if these terms are greeted with a collective roll of the eyes ("Try not to use the word *sustainable*," a wry friend told me), it's difficult to be a responsible modern gardener without using the right vocabulary. There are no good substitutes. So even though I have tried to use them judiciously, I've taken the use and exploration of these terms as a given in the writing of this book. This book can only scratch the surface of some of the more complicated, deep topics that it addresses, so I've included reading lists along the way for

readers who would like to learn more from the experts in these respective fields.

This book is an exploration of what I think are the gardens of the future. These gardens not only concern themselves with reaching their own best level of sustainability in water usage, plant choices, local ecology, and preservation of resources, but they are also aesthetically delightful. All the gardens I've included exhibit some degree of sustainability, be it large or small. Some aren't perfect. And though these garden makers' hearts may be in the right place, they may fall short on one aspect or another of the sustainable canon, so please be kind with your judgments.

I've also made the assumption that giving pleasure—visual, olfactory, and otherwise—is essential to any garden that we should wish to sustain. Thus I place special emphasis upon the aesthetic aspects of each project in these pages,

whether it be a seaside flower garden or a shady Brooklyn backyard. That is key for me as a gardener; what is a garden if it is not a thing of beauty? Of course, the definition of beauty itself can and does evolve. As I've matured as a gardener, and with the present renaissance of the green movement, I have formed new ideas of what makes an attractive garden in terms of design, plant selection, and materials. I photographed gardens in 10 cities across the country that reflect my current gardening experiences and those of dozens of professional and amateur gardeners making gardens that are beautiful and at the same time responsible. These people are moving things forward for tomorrow instead of just gardening for today or looking to the past. This book shows—I sincerely hope more than it preaches—how I think we should all strive to garden in the 21st century and for the future.

Garden Where You Live

PART I

CHAPTER 1

What's the Program?

ENTHUSIASTIC NEW GARDENERS often launch into the more decorative part of gardening (i.e., the planting of flowers) before giving the spatial design much thought. Ahead of plant selection, one of the most important lessons to learn when making a garden is to consider how each area is going to be used. Each defined space should have a purpose—what architects refer to as a program. Will you be eating outdoors? Will you be entertaining small groups of friends for dinner or having formal cocktail parties for work? Do you have kids and/or pets? Is there a quiet spot to escape from the kids with a drink or a book? How well do you like your neighbors? Can you create some sense of privacy? Ask yourself these important lifestyle questions to plan your valuable outdoor spaces most effectively and keep them from going unused, which is a waste of valuable time and money.

The Outdoor Room

Of course, the answers to many of the above questions will vary according to where you live. Speaking from personal experience as a native Texan, many residents of that state possess a seemingly innate desire to stay indoors. Perhaps it's the heat, but let's be frank—the weather in much of the state is temperate for a large portion of the year. To thwart that tendency at an Austin, Texas, garden, landscape designer Mark Word specifically added smart elements to entice people outdoors. The small walled courtyard of the newly built house is a stylized campground of sorts with simple painted wood furniture, a fire pit, and a small running "stream" (abstracted as a tiered steel fountain). This elemental

Even though scale is important in a smaller garden, the plant choices don't need to be sized small as well. Mark Word contrasted the large leaves of rice paper plant (*Tetrapanax papyriferus*) and plume poppy (*Macleaya cordata*) with a graceful shoestring acacia (*Acacia stenophylla*) in an Austin, Texas, garden.

Previous page: By using striking plant selections and simple materials, designer Mark Word turned the stark architecture of a courtyard in Austin, Texas, into a pocket garden of dramatic plants, a water feature, a seating area, and a fire pit.

Homeowner Dan Seaver, *opposite*, wanted a backyard that was more than just an ordinary patch of grass ringed with flowerbeds. He ended up with a multiuse space, *above*, featuring an elegant outdoor dining room, a vegetable garden, and a small bit of lawn for his daughter.

approach employs earth, fire, air, and water to transform what could otherwise merely be a pass-through space or, at its worst, a claustrophobic cell that never gets used. Now instead, it's a spot for evening drinks by the fire. Flowers in the graveled space, even plants themselves, are few—but it's still a garden in the classic sense. Word combined a few special selections—yellow abutilon with prehistoric-looking rice paper plant (*Tetrapanax papyriferus*), plume poppy (*Macleaya cordata*), and the twisted trunk of a slender shoestring acacia (*Acacia stenophylla*)—into a sculpture garden of bold plants. The splashing fountain, deep enough to sustain several hardy water lilies through the winter, drowns out street noise.

In a part of Venice, California, that is making the transition from modest midcentury bungalows to contemporary (but still small-scale) home remodels, Dan Seaver and his spouse, Will Speck, created a private backyard with an open-air dining room surrounded by gravel. Previously, the space was almost completely barren, so it was vitally important to inject some sense of spatial definition. Mark Tessier, their landscape architect, had the idea to add some truly green architecture—a shady grove of six African sumac trees (*Rhus lancea*). Their willowy leaves and slender reddish brown trunks form an airy canopy over an outdoor table where Seaver says it is cool and inviting on even the hottest day. The drought-tolerant, low-maintenance sumacs are evergreen but frequently shed their leaves, meaning they can be a bit messy. So you need to be either okay with a little regular sweeping or comfortable with a little naturalistic imperfection. There are just a few furnishings in this simple garden: a rustically modern wooden table, a stone sphere, and a shallow concrete birdbath. A small vegetable garden and a square of lawn for the couple's young daughter are the only parts of the property that require much in the way of regular water.

In Ojai, California, landscape designer Paul Hendershot makes gardens that gracefully borrow style and mood from parts of the world that share his hot dry climate—such as Provence, Italy, and Spain. In such locations, the sun is strong, shade is a necessity, and plants have to be tough and drought resistant. Outdoor dining and activities like bocce are essential parts of the lifestyle. For a home just outside the town of Ojai, Hendershot planted a dense canopy of fruitless mulberries (*Morus alba* 'Stribling') in a gravel terrace surrounded with clipped herbs and walls made of stone excavated on the site. The trees' dense leaves throw cool shadows over the dining area all summer. In the mild winter, the trees lose their leaves, allowing diners to bask in the sun, which is welcome by that time. Hendershot picked a fruitless variety to avoid the mess caused by the dark-staining berries and the visiting hungry birds that enjoy the fruit and spread the seeds far and wide.

Mind the Roots

Mulberries are fairly tolerant of drought once they get established, but be aware that their aggressive roots are large and shallow, so these trees shouldn't be placed near masonry or sidewalks. At a garden in Ojai, California, Paul Hendershot set up a watering system for the trees that irrigates them deeply once a week, keeping the roots from growing too near the surface. As is common in Europe, the trees are kept small and dense by pollarding them (pruning back their upper branches to the main set of limbs) once a year in late winter or early spring.

A surprisingly graphic approach can be seen in a garden created by designer Beth Mullins of Growsgreen Landscape Design for Tom Lakritz and Chris Wagner. The clients requested a unusual garden element for their small backyard in the Monterey Heights neighborhood of San Francisco: a labyrinth. In the past few years, these intricate garden features have become much sought after as meditative spaces. Often, the labyrinth is fairly large and situated as a destination out in a larger property to draw people away from the house and into another part of the garden. This 17-foot-wide design, inspired by the patterns found in San Francisco's Grace Cathedral and medieval churches like Chartres, takes up most of the backyard—that's quite a spatial commitment.

Opposite: Every outdoor room should have a well-considered purpose. Paul Hendershot created a family gathering place in sunny Ojai, California, under a cool canopy of fruitless mulberry trees. *Above:* At the request of her San Francisco clients, Beth Mullins designed a labyrinth of drought-tolerant grasses for their small backyard.

Mullins outlined her walkable design with clumps of Berkeley sedge (*Carex divulsa*) in gravel instead of calling for a tighter pattern mown in lawn or using more conventional hedges of yew or boxwood. The sedge labyrinth doesn't need much water, and Mullins says it requires clipping or a little thinning only three times a year, when it gets to be about 2 feet tall. This unusual garden element makes a graphic design for viewing from the house or the raised deck while satisfying its original function as a meaningful contemplative activity for the homeowners as they walk its course.

For clients in Brooklyn, Susan Welti and Paige Keck came up with a narrow sequence of garden rooms that makes a large but narrow backyard appear even larger. Nearest the house is an informal seating area, *above and opposite*. At the rear is a dining area and custom-designed playhouse, *below*.

A Multiuse Space

In Brooklyn, designers Susan Welti and Paige Keck of Foras Studio renovated an unhappy backyard dominated by a derelict lawn and a motley collection of overgrown shrubs. They replaced it with a stylishly modern family garden subdivided by stone pavers, a grove of trees, and a wooden boardwalk. That's a far cry from what Gigi Sharp and George Gilpin saw when they bought the place in 2003. At that time, the lawn was a muddy, mosquito-ridden mess. Even in its compromised condition, the narrow backyard was an enormous draw for the couple with two young sons: The end-to-end double lot, measuring 20 by 80 feet, stretches from street to street, with a garage in the rear.

Though the house is a classic 19th-century brownstone, Welti and the owners wanted to modernize the garden so that it would better suit the style of the new concrete, glass, and metal addition that the couple had built on the back of the house. The long, narrow garden already had a small patio and several changes in its levels, a feature that Welti found very appealing since a completely flat space doesn't hold as much design interest. In this case, the small series of grade changes fell in just the right proportions for the designer, so she kept them, knowing that this simple decision would save a lot of the expense and environmental damage of regrading the site and hauling away tons of soil and debris. She replaced the outmoded railroad ties that had formed the most prominent low wall near the house with poured concrete and replaced the soggy, poorly draining patch of lawn with a small grove of trees. Welti feels that all too often, homeowners with outdoor space have a strong, almost innate, desire to try to grow bright green lawns. But in a shady urban situation where the soil and drainage are often questionable, it takes an inordinate amount of effort (including the use of artificial fertilizer and chemicals) to get turf to be pristine. In

Dividing a Space Makes It Seem Bigger

Garden designers have long known something that seems counterintuitive: Taking a small space and separating it into different, discrete areas makes it seem larger. A tall hedge, a wall, a fence, or an opaque clump of shrubs keeps a visitor from seeing the whole view at once, even if it is a relatively compact space, *above*. Each turned corner provides a new discovery: a private dining area or a secluded seating area with a bench and a fountain. Nothing is more boring than to look out the back door and see the whole yard spread out to be viewed at a glance. What's the point in going outside to take a look around when there is nothing to go around?

Planting Small

Though the plantings in the Sharp and Gilpin yard look fully mature now, this was hardly a garden with instantaneous results. Since most of the container-grown plants were purchased in small sizes ranging from 5 to 10 gallons, the garden required several years to reach its desired state—an approach that takes patience and trust on the part of the homeowner. Partially this decision was based on the realities of the budget, but Keck (and many notable designers) feels that most plants succeed better when put in young so that they can acclimatize more easily to their new surroundings without the abrupt shock of a full-grown transplant.

most cases, she advises her clients to do without traditional grass. With the lawn removed, the replacement surfaces—groundcover plants, pavers, wood boardwalk, and river stones—help move the once neglected garden into the new century.

Everyone involved agreed that the new yard shouldn't be too precious or pristine. Instead, they wanted an easy, low-maintenance atmosphere—a place where the family could relax, entertain, and spend hours outdoors. Welti transformed the formerly disused space into three highly usable family-oriented areas. A bluestone patio, furnished with vintage outdoor chairs, is a relaxed spot to hang out with friends before dinner. A dining table and chairs sit on a wooden platform partially obscured by a multilevel green barrier of low boxwood, a higher hedge of yew, and a small grove of Japanese maples. The trees create an important sense of enclosure and privacy. Welti was keen on imagining how the family would move back and forth through the yard—hence the cedar boardwalk that unites the different living areas.

With its reliance on plant-based architecture of trees, long-blooming perennials, and shrubs, the garden is also inexpensive to maintain. Gilpin says he enjoys the small amount of yard work that's required, only a little raking of the planting beds and sweeping of the terrace and boardwalk once a month or so. Welti and Keck visit twice a year to check on how things are growing, determining which plants may need replacing or rejuvenating and giving the hedges a trim. Most blissfully, there is no need for the weekly invasion of the usual sort of mow-and-blow maintenance company that arrives loaded with power tools, cuts the lawn, blasts the grass clippings all over the place before making a hasty exit. That's probably the most valuable and serene design feature an urban garden can have.

A stone terrace, the most open area of the garden, sits just behind a sleek new addition by Joseph Tanney at Resolution: 4 Architecture. Farther back, a dining table and playhouse are screened from the house by a grove of Japanese maples, *below.*

Gardening with Kids (for Modernists)

Los Angeles landscape designer Judy Kameon and her husband, Erik Otsea, aren't the sort of parents who go to great lengths to alter their houses or gardens for the sole sake of their child. Their steep garden in the hilly Elysian Park

neighborhood of Los Angeles would make many an overprotective parent reach for his or her antianxiety medication. Besides the large, sharp-tipped agaves and a variety of changes in level delineated by walls and concrete steps, there isn't a patch of lawn or a jungle gym in sight. In this case, the dramatic topography has become a playscape in itself—and

Ah, California. Landscape designer Judy Kameon and her family, *left,* live as much outdoors as in their Los Angeles house. The fairly steep garden is made of terraces traversed by steps that pass under a giant pepper tree. The most radical transformation in the property occurred when the couple built a larger, modernist house designed by architect William Nicholas of Nicholas/Budd Architects on the site of a former artist studio. Instead of tearing down their 1928 stucco bungalow, *opposite,* they decided to keep it as a guesthouse.

one that is perfectly safe. "My feeling from the start was that if Ian grew up in this garden, he would know how to act in it," Kameon says of her son. And she has been proved right.

The situation might be different if the family had moved to this wilder kind of garden from a normal flat yard with a grassy lawn. "I've overheard Ian warning his little friends who visit, 'That plant is spiky.' He's never had anything more than a tumble or a scrape, same as any other play area," Kameon says. Other children require more careful supervision when they come over for play dates or parties, since they find the walls and stonework irresistible for climbing. Though the varied landscape is completely enthralling to kids, it was originally designed only with adults in mind. Kameon was single and an artist when she bought the property 20 years ago. Its central but off-the-beaten-path neighborhood near wooded Elysian Park had been isolated from the rest of the city by the construction of several freeways and Dodger Stadium. Like many properties in neglected neighborhoods, the sloped site on a quiet side street was weedy and dusty. It was blessed, however, with the large, spreading limbs of a California pepper tree (*Schinus molle*) that still serves as the centerpiece of the garden.

Kameon started by terracing the yard and installing walls, but she needed a way to traverse the steep grade from her house at the bottom of the long property to what would become her home office up at the rear. The designer marked the planned route by scattering a bag of chalk on the ground where she wanted to install a series of steps made of inexpensive landscape ties (beams of lumber similar to larger, rougher railroad ties used to retain raised beds or outline planting areas). Years later, the rustic ties were replaced in the same location with concrete steps inlaid with pebbles. "At the time I started gardening, I thought you needed to terrace everything in a hillside to get flat

A huge old California pepper tree original to the property shelters a flat terrace covered in decomposed granite where the family can have a large group of friends and neighbors over for dinner. Concrete-and-pebble steps lead down to the swimming pool through primeval-looking plantings of agave, acanthus, cordyline, and weeping bamboo.

spaces for planting," Kameon says. "But now I don't. Filling the slope with the right kind of plants achieves the same purpose."

The future garden designer got her gardening education here, one that would lead her to start her own business, Elysian Landscapes, in 1996 and to join an influential group of like-minded LA plant fanatics called "the Germinators" in 1998. Over the subsequent years, she has made sure that every part of the garden has a distinct purpose and personality by employing different materials in each. Behind the bungalow, a small area of artificial lawn and an outdoor couch inspires Sunday newspaper reading or maybe a catnap. Several years ago, Kameon replaced the gravel that was originally there with SynLawn, which gives Ian a

flat, easy place to play and drive his toys around. "I just can't justify having real lawn in LA," she explains. The flagstone area around the circular pool (which is covered with a safety net until Ian is older) is for lounging and parties. One level up, a flat, circular area covered with crushed decomposed granite can host seated dinner parties under vintage metal lanterns hung from the wide branches of the pepper tree. Up at the top of the property, a gravel space under a large metal arbor once supported a hammock; now it's furnished with hoop chairs and outdoor tables by Plain Air, a line of contemporary outdoor furniture designed by Kameon and her husband.

At home and in her design work, however, Kameon isn't always a stickler when it comes to issues like native plants or some of the orthodox aspects of xeriscaping. "I can't say that this garden is as low water as it could be,"

she admits, noting that she began working on the garden quite a few years ago, when the area's water crisis was not as apparent. "But for something that is so densely planted, it does pretty well." When the city imposed mandatory water restrictions recently due to severe drought, Kameon adhered to the schedule "even though things got pretty crunchy by the end of the summer." Since then, most of the plants have rebounded well, and any that didn't make it probably won't be replaced. "In our business, we just don't use high-water plants like ornamental gingers, hard-core tropicals, or even most roses anymore," she says. "But there are some unexpected drought-resistant plants like bamboo and certain tough roses like 'Iceberg' that don't need much water once they're established." At home she is constantly reevaluating and editing her plantings to be lower maintenance as well, each year replacing problem

varieties that require too much attention with more self-sufficient species.

The family lives indoors and out in an almost seamless way. "Ian's in the garden all the time, and we have our little picnics on our fake lawn," Kameon says. The relaxed attitude of this theatrical garden with its giant cactus, towering bamboo, and dramatic topography is an ideal spot for adults. But for a child, it's also a playground that exercises a fertile imagination, giving Ian what promise to be lifelong memories of a charmed childhood spent clambering over an improbably jungly garden in the dry hills of Los Angeles.

Instead of formal hedges, large clumps of loose-looking plants divide Judy Kameon and Erik Otsea's garden, *opposite*. From the top of the property, *above*, you can see through a transparent section of the house to a lower terrace and a patch of artificial turf, where their son can play, *right*.

A Garden of Utility

How can flowers be utilitarian? Frances Palmer, a successful potter, creates vessels that are as much inspired by the forms of nature as by Greek pottery and Japanese ceramics, so her idyllic Connecticut cutting garden is more than just a place of beauty. The tall, elegant stems of her prized dahlias, sunflowers, and self-sown annuals are the inspirations behind many of her new designs, all of which she throws and fires in her large barn studio behind the cutting garden. The relationship between what goes on in the garden and what goes into the kiln is almost symbiotic, as she cuts plants to take inside to study or arrange in the new vases. She then photographs the arrangements for her own records and publicity before shipping the one-of-a-kind vases to her clients. Sometimes, when a favorite variety is about to bloom, Palmer creates a special vase just to hold the new flower as it opens. She also grows tomatoes, berries, and herbs for the table, though these often find their way into floral arrangements as well. Palmer's main focus, however, is dahlias—more than 100 kinds. Perhaps because her work is about shape and form, she has been drawn to these intricate, graphic blossoms for the past 15 years. They come in balls, spikes, pompons, pinwheels, huge "dinner plates," and the simple single-petaled shapes of the true species. Their colors are found on the warm end of the spectrum (there are no true blues), so all the reds, pinks, magentas, reddish purples, molten blacks, yellows, bronzes, and oranges blend well together: There's no need to segregate the colors. The tall plants create a vivid jungle by the end of the season in September.

In her Connecticut cutting garden, Frances Palmer, *opposite*, gathers armfuls of colorful dahlias to make arrangements and to inspire the ceramic vessels she forms in her barn studio, *above*.

In Frances Palmer's cutting garden, flowers are grown almost like vegetables. *Above*, the simple plots are bare before they are planted up in spring, and in full bloom at the end of the season, *below*.

Overall, Palmer doesn't worry about a tidy visual statement. She enjoys her flower plot in its wild and unruly state. "It reminds me of the Alice in Wonderland garden that I remember from childhood," she says. She extracts the weeds only if they get really out of hand—otherwise they generally get a pass—and errant annuals are encouraged to volunteer in the pea gravel paths that run between the four main square beds. It isn't until visitors arrive that Palmer considers what a stranger might think of the glorious chaos—but as every gardener knows, there are always ready excuses for that. There is, however, one element of control that is unavoidable and perhaps even welcome. Every fall, the garden reaches a crescendo that is wiped clean by frost, when all the tender plants die back to the ground. She then lifts and labels the dahlias, storing them in sawdust and newspaper in the basement until the following spring, when they are planted in bare beds once the danger of frost has passed. Meanwhile, tall sunflowers, nicotiana, zinnias, cosmos, and sweet peas self-seed outdoors where they fall—or new seeds are planted in the spring.

Palmer keeps her garden productive and on a manageable, personal scale. It's entirely organic, as if it were a vegetable plot, and like a vegetable garden, it isn't in any way a xeriscape and requires supplemental irrigation. However, even though she lives in a fairly rain-rich climate, watering is kept to a minimum except during the hottest part of the year or during the rare drought. Palmer composts all her kitchen scraps for the beds, which may explain the gargantuan size of her plants. She says that, depending on the variety, a happy dahlia tuber may increase in size tenfold in one season. Friends all over the country are eager participants in her dahliamania, since the plants love to be divided each year.

In Palmer's garden, the beauty of the rustic flower plot comes from the sheer volume of tall annuals and self-sown annuals that tower above the deer fencing.

Los Angeles gardener Tara Kolla, *left*, launched a business growing cut anemones, sweet peas, and ranunculus right in her own backyard to sell at local farmers' markets—but not without difficulties. Along the way, she was allowed by a gracious customer to expand her growing space to the empty kitchen garden of a nearby historic estate in Silver Lake with amazing views of the city, *opposite*.

A Garden for Profit

Who could take issue with a backyard full of flowers? Why would anyone complain about neat organic plots of harmless anemones and ranunculus or fragrant tunnels of sweet peas? What grinch could want to put a stop to such beauty, and by court order no less? Los Angeles resident Tara Kolla knows the answers all too well. She had been growing those flowers in her Silver Lake backyard and selling them at local farmers' markets for 7 years. Then catastrophe struck several years ago, when several neighbors decided that Silver Lake Farms, her small commercial enterprise, was spoiling the quality of their neighborhood. So they reported her to the city's department of building and safety because she was selling her homegrown flowers at local farmers' markets. After a lot of research, Kolla determined that the law her neighbors invoked was a 1946 building code that addressed the concept of truck gardening—defined as pertaining explicitly only to the growing and selling of vegetables for market, not flowers.

She weighed her options. Option one was to apply for a variance for her own property, but that wouldn't help anyone else around the city in her situation, and Kolla, being fiercely community minded, did not want to just fend for herself. In addition, such a process would costs thousands of dollars that this small business owner did not readily have. Option two was to continue her habits and face a fine of $1,000 or 6 months in jail, "which frightened the bejeezus out of me," says Kolla. Option three was to change the law, and option four was to stop urban flower farming all together. She chose number three.

Kolla soon found herself in the position of being a reluctant urban farming activist in the local press, at some times furious and driven to win back her rights and at other times debilitated and depressed by the struggle of it all. After months of back-and-forth negotiations with her neighbors and the city, Kolla decided to pursue option three and strive to alter the building code. She and several other like-minded Los Angelenos who were involved with organizations like Urban Farming Advocates and Homegrown Evolution worked hard for many months to pass the Food & Flowers Freedom Act (posted online at www.urbanfarmingadvocates .org). Through a lot of hard work, the ad hoc consortium got the law changed in their favor.

Kolla knew that she couldn't have done it by herself, even with the solid support of her husband, Beat Frutiger. "I am too emotional on this subject to interface directly with the city bureaucracy," she admits. Meanwhile, as she waited for the slow legal wheels to turn, Kolla organized a CSA (community-supported agriculture) project with a nearby farmer, a venture that allows subscribers to order a weekly share of his produce. But for Kolla, the CSA is not a singular goal—now she also gets the chance to resurrect her backyard cut-flower operation and replant the growing fields that she

Tara Kolla learned the hard way how to have a successful organic growing business at home while dealing with the demands of city codes and concerned—and not always cooperative—neighbors.

had begun in an old kitchen garden at the Paramour, a nearby historic estate where the owner has generously allowed Kolla to garden. "I've received a flood of support from people," she says. "Evidently, there are a lot of people out there who hope urban farming for food or flowers can really work." Thanks to her seemingly inexhaustible spirit and the encouraging support of a like-minded community of friends and strangers interested in starting green businesses in their own backyards, Kolla is getting her livelihood back one beautiful flower stem at a time.

Tara's Advice for Starting a Backyard Business

- Install a water utility submeter for your garden to help separate business expenses from normal household water usage.

- To grow good produce, maximize available sun by picking a south- or west-facing exposure.

- Plan easy access to the growing beds so that crops can be harvested and transported without disturbing the neighbors.

- Scout local farmers' markets first before selecting your cash crop and grow plants that fill an empty niche in the market.

- Check local zoning regulations and register your business with the proper agencies. Also contact your state department of agriculture to get certified to become a market grower.

CHAPTER 2

What's the Weather?

MOST GARDENERS HAVE water issues these days—either there's too much or too little. With all the unpredictability of our changing climate, it seems that the only constant most US gardeners have had over the past several years is the element of surprise. Where I live in the Northeast, some recent growing seasons have been wetter and cooler than normal, bringing scourges like powdery mildew and the late blight that threatens the region's tomato harvest. At those times, it's as though a soggy blanket has been thrown over the whole season. Of course, beachgoers and gardeners may moan and feel inconvenienced, but the real damage comes at the expense of the farmers who depend on warm temperatures and predictable rainfalls to get their crops to maturity and out of the ground. But then the next summer, everything might change as early and unpredictable heat waves bake the region and seem to ward off rain like a giant umbrella. Suddenly, a renewed focus on gardens that conserve water is necessary.

Gardens of Stone and Water

For all our concerns about saving water, however, strictly speaking there's no such thing as truly dry gardening. Even in the most successful xeriscapic garden, where the admirable goal is to use species that will thrive without much supplemental irrigation, plants still need natural precipitation. But sometimes, rain doesn't come. In areas like Southern California or parts of the Southwest like Texas that have been severely affected by drought, gardeners may go without rain for many months, and even a tried-and-true low-water garden will suffer without relying on municipal water.

Los Angeles, seen here from the top of Mulholland Drive, relies heavily on imported water for its lushly planted backyards and gardens. Many forward-thinking gardeners in that city are reconsidering what plants might better suit their desert climate.

When Texas native Christy Ten Eyck returned to live in her home state after 22 years of designing gardens in Phoenix, she couldn't help but look at her new Austin garden through the lens of her experiences trying to grow plants in Arizona's harsh, arid climate. When most people start a new garden, they think first about what they want to plant and then head to the nursery. Ten Eyck, however, first evaluated the underlying systems of her property to determine what elements needed altering, such as its drainage and soil conditions. The right plant choices came second.

The ranch-style 1950s limestone house that she and her husband, Gary Deaver, bought in 2006 had a large lot shaded by the graceful branches of native oak trees but no real garden to speak of. The property, which was formerly owned by well-known Texas artist Julie Speed, was full of the laid-back bohemian charm that Austin is famous for, but Ten Eyck felt that several of its more conventional aspects had to go immediately. "Right out front, there was this enormous St. Augustine lawn," Ten Eyck says. "And running through the middle of that was a big, circular driveway, which is one of my pet peeves. I don't like looking out of my house right at the car." She was also shocked to discover how swiftly the storm water washed down the yard's fairly steep 8-foot grade change and out into the street. Unable to regrade the yard substantially because of potential damage to the sensitive oaks, she removed the turf grass and the asphalt driveway in the front and made a rain garden. Inspired by Native American farming practices she learned in Arizona, in

Landscape architect Christy Ten Eyck used many of the lessons she learned gardening in Arizona when she renovated her new garden in Austin, Texas. The centerpiece of the gravel garden is an overflowing and circulating trough fountain constructed of board-form concrete. Its blue water bubbles mysteriously, very much like the nearby aquifer-fed public swimming pools at Barton Springs and Deep Eddy. The fountain is surrounded by a small grove of native possumhaw (*Ilex decidua*), *above*, whose graceful brindled trunks appear even more elegant juxtaposed against the stark background of gravel.

which a series of arced catch basins slow down runoff and trap water in small pools that then slowly soak into the soil, Ten Eyck constructed check dams from stone pieces removed during the renovations on the property. She amended the plantable pockets with compost so the soil would better hold water and allow for a new garden of Texas natives and even a lush grove of tomato plants. The Hill Country landscape in and around Austin, known geographically as karst for its soluble and pockmarked limestone bedrock, can be problematic for growing nonnative plants. The area's thin layer of soil sits on top of the porous stone, which absorbs water like a dry sponge, wicking it down to enormous aquifers that supply spring water to the area's many natural pools and lakes. As any Austinite will tell you, responsible water usage is of increasing importance, since the once plentiful underground reservoirs have become depleted by overdevelopment and drought.

While addressing the water issues, Ten Eyck and her husband also wanted to do away with a 6-foot-high stone wall that blocked their front yard from the street—especially since it was the only one of its kind on their block. "I wanted to create a sense of privacy with groups of plants instead of tall walls. It's much more welcoming." The choice of imported Colorado river stone in the wall felt incongruous, especially in a region known for its beautiful native limestone. Ten Eyck felt guilty, however, hauling away the valuable material. "I hate the idea of generating trash and debris," she says. "Of course, sometimes it's unavoidable." Luckily, once the wall was dismantled, the landscape contractor was happy to take away the unwanted stone for other projects.

Since her arrival, she has made her new West Austin home into a laboratory for her design business, which has

Previous page: In her front yard, Christy Ten Eyck removed a huge swath of St. Augustine lawn and replaced it with a stepped series of check dams inspired by Native American examples from the Southwest. Shown here soon after installation, the stone arcs catch the available rainfall and keep the valuable water from pouring out into the street. *Above and opposite:* A year later, the previously bare stone arcs are full of thriving native plants like bamboo muhly grass (*Muhlenbergia dumosa*) and a small vegetable plot of herbs and tall tomato plants. The crushed stone front walk curves elegantly from the street up the incline to the house.

offices in both Austin and Phoenix. Right in her own back-yard, she can experiment with a new palette of Texas native plants while trying to reduce water usage with techniques imported from the desert. In addition to the large front yard, there is a small strip between the main house and the rear guesthouse/studio and a large side yard with a lawn under an imposing oak tree. The in-between strip had previously been used for an unsuccessful vegetable and flower garden. Once Ten Eyck started to dig around a little, she realized why the garden was struggling: It was situated atop a shelf of chalky limestone. The stony space flooded during heavy rainstorms, pouring water into the nearby studio. Finding it impossible to do much in the way of planting, she excavated the top part of the stone shelf and regraded the problem area into a gravel courtyard. True to her desire to avoid sending heavy materials to the dump, Ten Eyck reused every bit of broken-up limestone and excavated soil, moving most of it into the front yard to construct the terraces and check dams.

Ten Eyck stuck primarily to Texas or southwestern natives for her yard, focusing on choices that would reward her appreciation of the passing seasons so absent in Phoenix. The possumhaws show off red berries for much of the winter, and the purple wisteria-like blossoms of the Texas mountain laurel (*Sophora secundiflora*) fragrantly announce the arrival of spring. She planted violet-fruited American beautyberry (*Callicarpa americana*), several kinds of salvias, red Turk's cap (*Malvaviscus arboreus*), and fluffy bamboo muhly grass (*Muhlenbergia dumosa*). She was also eager to try out some native fruits such as Mexican plums (*Prunus mexicana*) and Texas persimmons (*Diospyros texana*), which she says feed the local bird population.

After all the renovations, both indoors and out, Ten Eyck and her family enjoy the various garden areas all year long. The garden's first real summer was challenging, with an extended period of crippling heat and extreme drought, but the garden survived well with minimal use of drip irrigation. "Even on the hottest days, we live outdoors, especially in the evenings," Ten Eyck says. "And to be honest, I love to spend a little time raking the gravel. I find it all very relaxing."

The New Cottage Garden

Nantucket is better known for its beautiful flower gardening than its xeriscaping. Most yards feature white picket fences and classic cottage garden plants that thrive in the island's relatively mild, but summertime-dry, maritime climate. Connie Umberger, a longtime resident of the island, had previously owned a large, multiacre property but decided a few years ago that she wanted to scale down, so she bought a historic 17th-century house in town. There, she has made a charming garden of far-flung influences that still manages to look right at home in this fairly traditional town—almost as if it were the home of a world-traveling sea captain who had finally come to settle down.

Umberger began by removing the lawn in the back-yard, which was originally just a patch of grass and a huge pear tree. "I think it's silly to have much lawn here," she says, having no desire to mow or deal with the extensive watering grass requires during the island's dry spells. She terraced the slope into two flat areas with a low stone wall and made a gravel flower garden that mixes formal and informal planting styles with aplomb. Six silver willows (*Salix alba* 'Sericea')

By adding a long copper rill of circulating water, a covered swing seat, and lots of gravel, Connie Umberger transformed her once ordinary grassy backyard in Nantucket into a boldly eccentric interpretation of a conventional flowery cottage garden with vaguely Chinese overtones.

The Umberger garden is full of quirky details. *Above*, a fenceless gate. *Opposite, clockwise from top left:* The unusual *Echinacea* 'Pink Double Delight' mixes with drumstick allium; small waterfalls step down the subtle slope of the yard; ordinary plastic pots make a grand statement when painted a vivid scarlet; an ornate water spout is a source of the rill.

An Island Cottage Garden Plant List

Drumstick allium (*Allium sphaerocephalon*)
Weeping brown sedge (*Carex flagellifera*)
Teasel (*Dipsacus fullonum*) (*above*)
Echinacea 'Pink Double Delight'
Helenium 'Moerheim Beauty'
Helenium 'Rubinzwerg'
Helenium 'Sahin's Early Flowerer'
Red-hot poker (*Kniphofia uvaria*)
Opium poppy (*Papaver somniferum*)
Lavender cotton (*Santolina chamaecyparissus*)
Lamb's ears (*Stachys byzantina*)
Verbena bonariensis

trimmed into mopheads and a series of cylindrical boxwoods provide the necessary structure to keep the loose cottagey planting looking smart. She also reinterpreted the flowery Nantucket style with a clashing scheme of hot pink, purple, mauve, orange, and yellow worthy of a chic David Hicks interior. Well-chosen shades of flowering perennials mix with more fleeting annuals. Umberger loves how many of the plants self-seed so readily in the gravel (and also how easy the blanket of small stones makes it to spot and pull up weeds).

Most surprising of all, this lively planting only gets watered once a week during summer, yet it feels far from dry or arid. A central rill of water runs from a small spout in the stone wall down to the far end of the garden, providing the garden with movement and sound. A copper lining holds the water in the otherwise porous concrete form. The rill makes the space seem longer, as the water trickles over a series of tiny waterfalls to an eye-catching swinging bench at the far end of the garden. A mélange of historical influences seems to be Umberger's goal as she mingles varied objects from her collections to ornament the garden, including architectural fragments, stones that she finds interesting, animal statuary, and several willow obelisks for vines. "I like to use what I have," she says. "So I brought all the loose bricks that I could with me from my old house."

Umberger confesses that she has wondered from time to time if her garden design should be more colonial or obedient to a particular Nantucket style. Her misgivings are unwarranted. With verve and imagination, she has admirably imported stylistic influences without any need for justification.

Umberger's collecting instinct strays out from the inside of her antique-filled house, *opposite, clockwise from top left*: a cloud-clipped juniper next to a well-weathered half door, figurative and floral architectural fragments, and willow vine tepees topped with whimsical red ceramic caps.

Rain Gatherers

The goal of permeability is to keep the water, when and if it comes, on-site instead of allowing it to flow off-site into the gutter and the storm drain. At its simplest, this can be accomplished by sluicing the drainage off the roof through gutters and pipes into rain barrels or nearby planting beds. Just a few blocks from the ocean in Los Angeles, Jeff Pervorse of Bent Grass Landscape Architecture made a simple garden with more complexity than is immediately apparent. For this project, the storm water from the house and the hard surfaces in the garden flows down to the lowest part of the property, a sunken outdoor dining area. There it falls into an unobtrusive drainage hole and an underground cistern, where the water can seep into the surrounding soil. Here, permeability is Pervorse's design focus, influencing his choice of materials. The garden's low walls are made of gabions—stone-filled metal cages most often used in erosion control and engineering projects—which help diffuse the flow of water. In the past several years, gabions have become fashionable building elements in contemporary architecture. Pervorse uses them in both the back and front yards as a way to define different areas. Instead of a taller, more solid wall, they give an implied sense of separation that works well in the small yard. Natives such as red-trunked madrone (*Arbutus* 'Marina'), scarlet California fuchsia (*Epilobium* 'Catalina'), and several western redbud trees soften the edges and make a graceful counterpoint to what some might consider industrial materials unsuited to a garden.

A fairly conventional lot in Venice, California, became an exercise in rainwater runoff control and permeability for Jeff Pervorse. He designed the garden so that water flows over the roof and hard surfaces of the newly constructed house into a small drain at the lowest point of a sunken dining area, *opposite top*. Gabion walls, native grasses, and red-barked California madrones, *left*, enhance the graphic lines.

Handling the runoff from excess rain is a big concern in the Bay Area as well, which is dry for part of the year and often wet for the rest. At a large property in Tiburon owned by an art collector couple, James Lord and Roderick Wyllie of Surface Design made a long rain-catching ravine filled with smooth stones. Lined with clumps of *Pennisetum* 'Little Bunny' grass, a selection reported not to be a problematic self-sower like other fountain grasses, the rain garden doesn't try to look too natural but instead abstracts the idea of a common roadside culvert into a piece of land art. Any excess storm water that flows from the mossy slope above is diverted down the ravine to be absorbed into nearby garden beds. At the other end of the house, a highly permeable walkway of diagonally staggered stone strips interspersed with low groundcovers and stones ambles through a forest of bamboo and shrubs.

On a large property near San Francisco, Roderick Wyllie and James Lord constructed three different versions of permeable systems and walkways that can handle large amounts of rain without sending the runoff into the surrounding storm drain.

CHAPTER 3

Which Plant Where?

TO BE SUSTAINABLE, a garden doesn't have to be reduced to its most basic essentials of only a few staunch plants marooned in bare plots of stone or sand. If you like to grow flowers, then I hope you will. If you want to have a plant-intensive garden in which you cheerfully spend your evenings and weekends at work in your flowerbeds, then by all means do. I love flowering plants myself; in fact, I couldn't live happily without them. The main question to ask yourself if you want to be an environmentally conscious gardener (i.e., one who strives to sustain your surroundings rather than deplete them) is this: What kinds of garden plants are suitable for where and how you live?

Redefining the Plant Palette

We have a lot of garden baggage to deal with. It's time to shake off our outmoded ideas about what plants make a good garden, along with concepts that most of us have toted around since childhood about what a real garden looks like. The first colonists not only brought food plants to America but also imported their countries' long-established ideas of what makes a garden genuine, authentic, or at the very least pretty. These inherited notions have lingered ever since, and though such traditions have worked pretty well in New England, the standard became harder to satisfy as our population moved south and west. Think of the traditional plantings of begonias, impatiens, and petunias found in many municipal squares and of all the resources it takes to keep them looking presentable. Even the White House, with its enormous lawns and frequently swapped-out flowerbeds, doesn't seem interested in making radical updates to the centuries-old planting style. Except for Michelle Obama's organic vegetable garden, there has been no obvious gesture made toward native plants or sustainable horticulture.

Los Angeles designer Barry Campion's planting style uses Mediterranean-climate plants like euphorbia or leucospermum the way a more conventional garden might include water-hogging roses, hydrangeas, and tropical annuals.

American garden books often make the same mistake. They treat the wide range of the nation's gardens as if they were all governed by the same conditions. For this book, I traveled the nation to talk to gardeners who could help me address the breadth and range of our nation's horticulture from many different perspectives. It's not easy to speak helpfully and with accuracy to everyone at once, especially since this is such a huge country with so many gardening zones—British garden writers have it much easier. I needed to acknowledge that there are places where billowing masses of old-fashioned summer flowers seem to grow easily, almost as if they were in a classic English garden—Nantucket and Aspen come to mind. On the other hand, there are plenty of areas, like parts of the Southwest,

where the hot summers and the lack of water conspire to create an environment in which traditional flower borders are at best a vain struggle. A flexible mind-set is required to recognize what nature will allow us to grow in our area and to give up the struggle to grow plants that don't wish to grow for us no matter how strongly we urge them.

Take a moment to consider what grows well for you without a lot of coddling, chemicals, or excess water and fertilizer. If you're a new gardener and don't have a lot of knowledge, then just take a look around the neighborhood to see what succeeds on its own (being careful to recognize and avoid carefree weeds, of course). On the other hand, don't think you must use only natives or plants endemic to your region to be sustainable. A strict planting palette of natives is a fine goal, but I believe that gardening by its very definition is the act of modifying nature, and sometimes that entails growing things in places where they wouldn't normally exist. Suitability is crucial. If you have to work too hard to help something survive, perhaps it's simply not the right choice. Researching your plant selections is essential. Do an online background check to learn where a species that you'd like to grow originates. It doesn't make sense to grow a plant from the Amazonian rain forest in a water-starved place like New

Barry Campion's Venice, California, garden is full of unexpected surprises. *Opposite:* A rusty tricycle left decades ago by a friend is now parked under a staghorn fern, and a back fence is tinted emerald green. Nothing is discarded if possible; a fishpond, *above,* is surrounded by a low wall made out of the jackhammered bits of the former driveway. The distressed finish of an old porch glider, *below,* blends in with the metallic tones of a bromeliad collection started from a few cuttings.

Mexico, nor does it make sense to attempt a cactus garden in the winter wet of Seattle. On the other hand, gardeners in those parts of the world with a Mediterranean climate, such as California, parts of Australia and South Africa, and Chile, can easily swap exotic species with impunity. These guidelines won't stop a lot of hard-core gardeners from trying to push their climates to the edge like daredevils—it is perhaps part of human nature to want to fight Mother Nature just a little.

Of course, given enough resources, anything can be forced. I remember flying to El Paso for a visit to far West Texas. As you gradually descend for landing over that remote city, you see a regular patchwork of native scrubby sagebrush that dots the flat areas of white sand for miles. As you get closer to the airport, though, this natural landscape gives way to a grid of lush suburban backyards and turquoise pools interrupted by vivid green expanses of golf courses. I hope that if I lived in El Paso, I would embrace the beautiful plant material from the Trans-Pecos region and Chihuahuan Desert and not try to bring some misplaced version of a lawn-filled northeastern garden down to bake on the border.

Barry Campion's Plant Lover's Mix

Abutilon hybrids

Alstroemeria hybrids

Bromeliads

Cape honeysuckle (*Tecomaria capensis*)

Clerodendrum ugandense

Dudleya brittonii

Euphorbia characias wulfenii

Euphorbia rigida

Geranium 'Claridge Druce'

Jerusalem sage (*Phlomis fruticosa*)

Leucospermum 'Spider'

Manzanita (*Arctostaphylos* 'Pacific Mist')

Roses: climbing noisette and evergreen tea varieties

Variegated buckthorn (*Rhamnus alaternus* 'Variegata')

Yarrow (*Achillea* 'Gold Plate')

The Eclecticist

"I'm not a fussy person," Barry Campion says of her Venice, California, garden. The landscape designer bought the house decades ago in a part of town that was, and still is, known for a funky, artistic vibe. Over the years, Campion has moved to more of a native-plant palette even though her garden has by no means been a strict example of that concept. "I started my garden a long time ago," she says. "Natives weren't such a big topic then. But I still believe that LA is all about the mix, really." She emphasizes that a good strong design is crucial to pull off a big variety of species without making a visual mess and tends toward using appropriate Mediterranean species

with similar low-water needs. That hasn't stopped her, however, from including a few of her favorite old-fashioned climbing roses like 'Desprez à Fleur Jaune' and the thorny 'Phyllis Bide', which scramble over a large arbor of welded steel standing where the driveway used to be. "Once they're established, the roses really don't take much attention," Campion says. "Plus I have such a weakness for them."

To showcase such a wide-ranging selection of plants, Campion knew to give her garden structure by modifying its outdated hardscaping elements. She removed the harsh and impermeable concrete driveway by breaking it into pieces. The rough chunks (gardeners have coined the term "urbanite" for this material) were interspersed with gravel to create walkways

Barry Campion recently got rid of the last vestige of her lawn. She covered the grass with mulch and waited a season, allowing it to die and compost in place. She next to a wooden deck and an area of hexagonal pavers. She stacked more of the concrete pieces to form a low barrier around the garden's centerpiece—a 20-inch-deep fishpond filled with water plants. Objects that might normally seem unwanted are reused in this garden, since one of Campion's main goals is to avoid having usuable elements hauled off-site to the landfill.

Campion values her eccentric neighborhood for its small bungalows with their little patios and well-planted pocket-size gardens that are not overly fenced. But all that's changing as property values have gone up dramatically in recent years.

plans to enlarge the flowerbeds between the former lawn and fishpond and fill the middle area with a vegetable garden or a little meadow traversed by a path.

"Many of the older wooden houses are being replaced by big contemporary glass and concrete things, which are built right to the property line," she says. "They all look the same. It's a sad thing to see, that loss of character." Campion and her neighbors, with their artistically heterogeneous gardens, express a kind of originality formed in the freethinking California of the 1960s and 1970s. Hopefully, they will be able maintain themselves as oases of horticultural individuality and diversity during the current desire to keep up with the Joneses—no matter how conventional the Joneses may be.

Natives—A Strict Approach

A shift in the choice of species can make the switch from a standard suburban garden to a lower-water scenario even more accessible. For a front-yard flower garden in La Cañada Flintridge in Los Angeles County, Jeff Pervorse of Bent Grass Landscape Architecture selected a native plant palette that looks fairly conventional set in a wide, circular lawn ringed with flowerbeds. But on closer inspection, the flowerbeds are full of California natives that have evolved to handle the region's weather patterns of dryness balanced by often sudden winter downpours. It's a method of planting that follows the revolutionary principles of the state's native plant evangelists of the last century: nurseryman Theodore Payne and plant collector/author Lester Rowntree. The two horticultural authorities would have likely appreciated the garden's avoidance of imports like agapanthus, bird of paradise, and bananas in favor of a looser mix of regional penstemons, salvias, and poppies. The irrepressible Rowntree, one of my supreme garden heroes, wrote in her 1936 book *Hardy Californians,* "It is said that native California plants are hard to grow. They are—as long as we insist on putting the wrong plant in the wrong place." Perhaps she would have approved of the property's native lawn as well. San Diego bent grass (*Agrostis pallens* 'San Diego') requires much less water than ordinary turf and may be semidormant during summer droughts. Granted, it won't have the year-round bright emerald hue of a lawn planted with that ubiquitous Southern California favorite, Marathon sod, but in my opinion, the less a lawn looks like a golf course the better.

Opposite top: Near Los Angeles, Jeff Pervorse made an almost English-looking flower border strictly out of California species. *Clockwise from opposite bottom:* blue penstemon, white crepey-petaled matilija poppy (*Romneya coulteri*), and soft sunset orange sticky monkey flower (*Mimulus aurantiacus*).

Suitably Exotic

For those of us who don't live in California or the Southwest, these next two gardens—which exemplify the wonders a dedicated homeowner can create in a small space—would be hard to replicate. In Venice, a Los Angeles homeowner has filled his yard with succulents. This curbside garden is an eye-catching patched tapestry with different leaf colors and shapes of rounded kalanchoes, vivid crassulas, and spiny aloes and agaves. As in most cactus gardens, flowers are secondary, but there is a beautiful Chilean native to remark on. *Cistanthe grandiflora* has delicate magenta flowers that float above the blue green succulent leaves like butterflies.

Across town in Atwater Village, there's a showstopper of a turquoise house and cactus garden that's hard to miss. Surrounded as it is by neighboring yards of lawn and foundation shrubs, it's a quirky place. The more you look, the more you can appreciate the organic sense of design, with its carefully tended gravel beds edged with rounded stones and boulders. The tiny space supports an interesting variety of plant forms worthy of a sculpture gallery: skinny fans of ocotillo, bosomy barrel cactus, imposing stands of organ pipe cactus, and a changing display of vivid orange-flowering aloes. Granted, not everyone can fill their yards with subtropical cactus, but there is a lesson to be learned about replacing the front lawn with region-suitable plants and arranging them in such an artful way that not even the strictest, most conservative neighborhood association would complain. The benefits in terms of water usage, permeability, and appeal to wildlife and neighbors alike are inspiring in such unusual gardens.

Warm-climate gardeners are lucky to grow a remarkable number of tender species imported from locations with similarly mild weather conditions around the globe. A streetside planting, *opposite top*, overflows with tropical and subtropical succulents in the beneficent temperatures of Venice, California. On the other side of Los Angeles, clumps of cactus fill a front yard, *opposite bottom*. A carpet of succulents, *right*, relishes the fog in San Francisco.

Planting with Tradition

When I first started looking for projects to include in this book, I'll admit I was immediately drawn to the more modern, contemporary types of gardens. At first glance, they seemed much more sustainable in the way most of the media portrays the idea. I could easily discern in these projects a progression in the way gardeners are thinking about how plants, materials, and water should be used in the 21st century. Generally, we think of traditional flower gardens, with their pristinely clipped shrubs and high-maintenance borders, as being bigger consumers of all sorts of resources: money, labor, water, fertilizer, etc. But as my research progressed, I widened my scope to include certain, more classic flower gardens because I didn't want the book to be about only one style of garden. As a result, I found another whole category of gardens whose creators and designers desire to keep a sense of tradition and a bit of the romance of the past in their yards, often for very personal reasons. At the same time, they are striving in ways both large and small to incorporate forward-thinking ideas of responsibility.

Some of these gardeners have been developing their properties for decades, so their expertise, their interest in plant collecting, and their love of travel are revealed in every well-considered corner. They have worked long and hard on their gardens, and they're not about to chuck it all out to replace their flowerbeds with concrete pavers and a few cacti. I learned about how they've developed as gardeners and how

After experimenting with her Los Angeles garden, Suzanne Rheinstein has pared down the selection of plants to her absolute favorites. It's a move that may be as much about aesthetics as sustainability, but the end result is the same: less waste. Freed from trying to grow a lot of flowers in her shady yard and dry climate, she can focus her resources and energy on the pristinely clipped shrubs she loves.

they think about their yards now versus a decade or more ago. Where once they tried to grow everything under the sun, now they choose to specialize in only well-selected, time-proven favorites. Where before they wouldn't have given issues like water usage much of a second thought—perhaps because high water bills never needed to be questioned—now they may attempt to conserve for environmental reasons with or without municipally imposed restrictions. Whereas in the past no amount of gardening and yard work was too intensive, now they wish to scale back and *simplify* (a word I heard used by established gardeners from coast to coast).

This is especially true in places like Los Angeles that lately have had a tough run climatically. LA is a desert city, but you'd never know it as you drive through parts of town like Bel Air, Beverly Hills, and Hancock Park, where the wide streets are lined with large shade trees set in immaculate green lawns. Somewhere during its horticultural development, modern Los Angeles lost its way, and mass denial set in. Few gardeners wanted to acknowledge that they lived in a dry climate. They started to believe that their blessed mild temperatures, abundant sunshine, and as yet unrestricted water access would enable them to grow anything they desired. But now that the city's population has surpassed four million inhabitants during several years of crushing drought, it has become dramatically clear that all Los Angeles gardeners need to work within restrictions and limitations.

The dignified neighborhood of Windsor Square, among the greenest, leafiest parts of town, was developed in 1911 on part of one of the area's earliest Mexican land grants. However, it is difficult to identify any traces of dusty Rancho La Brea on these posh streets now. The area has a strong sense of tradition in its large houses and generous lots that reach far back from the broad streets. Most properties, at least the front yards, conform to the neighborhood's reserved style. But in the backyards, there is room to express more individualism and variety.

When Fred and Suzanne Rheinstein moved there 30 years ago, their back garden had a dated midcentury look that seemed at odds with the house's 1914 Georgian Revival exterior. Rheinstein, an influential interior designer and the owner of Hollyhock, an interiors store in West Hollywood, had the expertise to transform the space into something more evocative of her house's gracious past. At the same time, she wanted to make a "garden of memories" that harkened back to her childhood home in New Orleans but used plants suitable for Los Angeles. Rheinstein doesn't struggle with varieties that are hard to grow in Southern California, like lilacs or peonies. Instead, she concentrates on plants with strong shape and form that "happen to flower once in a while."

About 13 years ago, Rheinstein hired Judy Horton, a Los Angeles garden designer and a longtime friend, to help rethink and redesign the problematic backyard. They reduced the lawn, dividing it into several symmetrical, stylized pieces that resemble green carpets pierced by walkways made of stone pavers and some of the brick reclaimed from the patio. Rheinstein further reduced the lawn's square footage by adding a simple circular fountain that reflects light like a dark mirror in the center of the most open section of the garden. She knew from her visits to classic gardens in Europe that her garden could seem much larger if its views were partially obstructed and revealed gradually through fences and hedges designed to channel sightlines.

The evocative scents from a few favorite flowering plants like brugmansia fill Suzanne Rheinstein's garden and porch in the evenings, *opposite top*. The garden design is anchored by two main colors, chartreuse and Charleston green (a deep greenish black, which she used to paint the latticed wooden fence that shields the swimming pool), *opposite bottom*.

Small Evergreens for Shaping

Once established, these evergreens have the added benefit of not requiring excessive irrigation:

- Boxwood
- Dwarf olive (*Olea* 'Little Ollie')
- Dwarf spruce
- Germander
- Lavender
- Myrtle
- Rosemary
- Santolina
- *Westringia fruticosa*

This garden is undeniably formal and cannot by the most generous definition be called low maintenance. Yet in a subtle but important way, Rheinstein has steadily pursued a path of simplifying and paring down. In this case, sustainability is a question of degree. She began her garden with organic practices and continues to strive to waste less time, money, and resources. The garden is designed to look good without much worry beyond regular clipping. She removed the raised flowerbeds and added areas of gravel to plant graphic arrangements of shrubs that give a sense of structure without being static. True, Rheinstein does want things just so.

Small balls of silver westringia and olive nestled among large square panels of boxwood in Suzanne Rheinstein's Provence-inspired garden were inspired by fashion designer Nicole de Vésian's Provençal garden.

Rheinstein has reduced her color scheme as well, removing extraneous flowering plants in favor of those special few that she can't live without. Camellias remind her of her hometown, and at every turn in her backyard, fragrance triggers memories. Vigorous carefree climbing roses—like 'Rêve d'Or', 'Jeanne d'Arc', and the Cherokee rose (*Rosa laevigata*), a robust 18th-century southern favorite—scramble up walls and over the roof. Rheinstein's garden is a serene escape for its hardworking owners and seems a world apart from the traffic on the busy nearby streets. Surrounded by the glow of the last rays of Los Angeles's cinematically golden sunsets, it's hard to believe that you are in a city garden surrounded by miles and miles of the second-largest metropolis in the United States.

A few traditional elements like a small lawn and select groupings of antique garden furniture still remain in Carolyn Bennett's Los Angeles garden, *left and above*. But these reside comfortably with a new, more climate-appropriate plant palette and inventive modern touches—such as a dark reflecting pool designed by Judy Horton.

Even the birds quietly hopping from branch to branch don't seem to want to disturb the garden's serenity.

Just a few blocks away, another forward-thinking garden sits behind a traditional Windsor Square house: However, this one surprises in a different way. Carolyn Bennett began making her garden 22 years ago, inspired by memories of the traditional Midwest gardens of her childhood. Like so many gardeners in the 1980s, she was guided by the English gardens of Gertrude Jekyll and Vita Sackville-West. Originally, her style was almost anachronistic: a flower garden of roses with a white picket fence in the romantic style of a 19th-century English cottage, where a wide variety of plants grow with abandon. But in 2002, when Bennett, a landscape historian and garden consultant, returned with her family from 6 years spent living in London, she looked hard at her backyard (now appearing decidedly more unromantic after several years under the care of renters) and asked herself why she was striving for a lush English garden in dry Southern California. "I wanted to embrace the subtlety of California's climate," she says. "We don't have four distinct seasons here, and there aren't the extremes in temperature. But we do have subtle changes to appreciate." Since her old garden used a lot of water, it no longer seemed appropriate, so Bennett decided to start fresh with a garden that would better suit her real climate rather than her imagined one. She reduced the amount of lawn, leaving only a small square at the rear of the property, and added species that reflect her Mediterranean-type setting.

Bennett recently removed the last of her roses, making her garden's conversion to LA's desert climate complete. Her new style of planting has done well through the recent and perilous droughts. But in the meantime, like her friend Suzanne Rheinstein, Bennett has created an eminently useful, restful—and still evocatively traditional—space, one in which beloved historical vocabularies fit comfortably in the new gardening style of Los Angeles. At all levels of the community, the residents of Los Angeles increasingly choose to conserve for reasons that go deeper than their pockets; along the way, many reap the delightful bonus of aesthetic rejuvenation as well.

A Water-Saving Cottage Garden in Los Angeles

Agave attenuata 'Nova'

Agave desmettiana

Artichoke (Cynara cardunculus)

Cardoon (Cynara cardunculus)

Blue sotol (Dasylirion wheeleri)

Euphorbia 'Black Bird'

Mediterranean spurge (Euphorbia characias wulfenii)

Fruitless olive (Olea europaea 'Wilsonii')

Helichrysum 'Limelight'

Lavandula 'Goodwin Creek Grey'

Jerusalem sage (Phlomis fruticosa)

Prostrate rosemary (Rosmarinus officinalis 'Prostratus')

Mexican sage (Salvia leucantha)

Salvia 'Black Knight' and 'Indigo Spires'

Blue chalk sticks (Senecio mandraliscae)

Woolly thyme (Thymus pseudolanuginosus)

Once an ersatz English cottage garden, Carolyn Bennett's new backyard plantings feature true desert plants such as a large, spherical dasylirion and several kinds of agaves. Mediterranean-climate plants like chalky blue succulents, salvias, and silver, self-seeded artichokes and cardoons line the edges of a path made of local Santa Barbara sandstone and give the garden a sense of looseness reminiscent of the foreign gardens she once tried to replicate.

The Unrestrained Garden

Alta Tingle, a Bay Area store owner who has made a successful career collecting and selling beautiful objects, has lived perched high up on the hills above Berkeley, California, for the past couple of decades. From the front of her house, sweeping views extend from Alameda Bay past downtown San Francisco to faraway Marin County several miles away. In back, the hillside comes abruptly down to the large back windows of her living room, with little room to spare. Tingle tends this highly sloped garden with a loose hand bordering on the wild, but indeed the back-door wilderness does possess underlying structure—and a lot of usefulness in the form of edible plants.

When the neighbors rebuilt their fence a few years ago, Tingle was inspired to tackle her own yard by adding a series of planting terraces. Her good friend, Austin landscape architect James David, redesigned the sloped space by terracing it with boards stabilized with spikes to form a series of stepped boxes that contain what she calls her "paradise garden." A great lover of food and cooking (it is Berkeley, after all), Tingle wanted to be able to walk outside and pick fruit from her citrus trees but at the same time keep a sense of wildness. Hidden among the shrubby, almost overgrown forest garden is a veritable orchard of Meyer and Eureka lemons, Bearss limes, kumquats, sour calamondins, and the newly trendy yuzu (or Japanese citron). Tingle uses a lot of lemons, the mild Meyers for cold dishes and the tart Eurekas for

In Alta Tingle's wildly planted garden in the hills above Berkeley, California, pathways of reused broken-up concrete, *top right*, snake through a collection of citrus trees, camellias, and sculptural objects like these blue ceramic globes by artist Bruno Kark, *opposite top*.

cooking. Anything that she can't use, she gives away to friends. Even with all this fertility, the garden is not water intensive. There is a drip irrigation system, but Tingle often turns it off since she doesn't want to use much water. Luckily, on the cool slope most of the plants do well without the supplemental irrigation.

Tingle's evident love of garden ornament may have originated at her Berkeley store, The Gardener, which she founded in 1984 and now has branches in San Francisco and Healdsburg. Her collecting eye is evident throughout the garden, where well-chosen objects punctuate the leafy slope. An elegant stone step that she is "99.9 percent sure came from Asia" marks the entry to an overgrown path. Nearby, vivid cobalt blue ceramic spheres by Bay Area ceramicist Bruno Kark cluster in one corner of the bank of plants. She moves the balls (and other ornaments) around the garden as she sees fit; currently, they fill a gap where she had to remove a phormium. Big, asymmetrical Asian pots are placed here and there. A tower of ceramic blocks by Mary Alison Lucas, another local artist, looks precarious but remains stabilized deep in the soil halfway up the slope. The small yard, with its jungle of water-conscious plantings and ornamental accents, has a natural, unforced eclecticism that a more manicured garden could never convey and exactly reflects its owner's wide-ranging interests and passions.

Alta Tingle's steep hillside garden forms a lush backdrop to the large rear windows of her 1960s redwood house. Groundcovers and vines fight it out among phormiums, agapanthus, and daylilies on the incline. A wooden enclosure on the right side almost obscures a small boxed-in kitchen garden of herbs, broccoli, passion fruit, and her favorite English peas. More cooking herbs and scented geraniums grow thickly in pots.

The Conscientious Nursery Owner

Let's say for a minute that you want to go into a green business, something that works with nature and the earth. What about owning a nursery? Doesn't it seem eco-friendly to help populate the earth with beautiful leafy plants? Well maybe, but one of the most responsible nursery proprietors I know, Flora Grubb, offers some honest concerns that even a weekend plant shopper should consider.

Grubb, owner of the forward-thinking Flora Grubb Gardens in San Francisco, feels that just the sheer volume of plants sold in a single season can become an environmental concern from the standpoint of waste. Though her nursery primarily sells drought-tolerant plants to a horticulturally savvy clientele, Grubb has to work hard to communicate with her customers to find out how many of the plants that leave her doors actually survive. "In most areas, people, especially those who are new to gardening, buy plants that initially need water twice or more a week," she says. "Then they get busy and forget to water and that plant dies."

Her sort of personal approach is reason enough to patronize independent nurseries instead of the big-box stores that sell their plants in the disinterested way that a centralized factory farm distributes its plastic packages of celery while undercutting the small local growers and distributors. There are other motivations for the gardener who wants to buy with a clear conscience. "People have a visceral reaction to a well-

San Francisco nursery owner Flora Grubb, *opposite left*, has a thriving business built on her reputation for horticultural savvy and sense of style. The semi-enclosed main section of the store, *opposite top*, is open to the elements for much of the year. An old car, *opposite bottom*, found on the site before construction, is now a planter. A silvery leucadendron, *above*, is one of several South African species for sale.

priced plant that's in full bloom, and you can't argue with that," Grubb says. "But it can be a very ugly story how they get those plants covered in perfect flowers." She says that ordinary potted nursery plants are sprayed with all sorts of chemical growth retardants and bloom enhancers to get them in just the right state for delivery on those first warm spring weekends. "That's not nature. It's a chemical bath. We don't buy that stuff or sell it." She observes that most nursery customers don't seem to realize the chemical input taking place for each plant that they buy. If it was going to be eaten, then they might show more concern.

Invasive plants are another big issue that concerns Grubb. She feels the online invasive plant databases cannot keep up with all the new species that are being introduced. There are a lot of plants whose ability to escape cultivation have not been studied yet, and there are other already popular types that may behave well in some parts of the country but will run wild under the conditions in her area. "We've had to stop selling Mexican feather grass, for example, even though it's one of our top sellers," she says. "At first we thought it was okay in our area, since we were selling it mainly to urban gardeners. But now it's seen out in waterways, and we don't want to be responsible for problems in the future." She is also concerned about all the new plants that are being invented and mass-produced through tissue culture. "They rush these things to sell them without waiting to see how they mature or perform," she says. "And that's driven by a market where everyone wants to have a new plant to sell every year." We, the customer, have more power than we think we do. It's up to us not to insist on an endless parade of novelty plants every season.

It must be difficult to be in a business that, as she says, is caught between a rock and a hard place when it comes to delivering a good product at a fair price while the large chain stores hold such market power. We would all be in a better place if nursery owners asked themselves hard questions and spoke their minds, as Grubb does. "I have a recurring nightmare where at the end of my life I go to a hell composed entirely of black plastic nursery pots," Grubb says. She realizes that even though there are biodegradable options for plant pots, packaging is one part of the nursery business that is resistant to change for both the sellers and the buyers. Of course at her nursery, customers can bring the empty pots back to be reused, but many don't. Once again, the burden falls on the consumer to make the right choices. Do that and the marketplace will hopefully follow suit.

In the Bay Area, Flora Grubb is blessed with a wealth of excellent local growers and mom-and-pop nursery operations. She says her primary goal—and that of her staff—is to get the right plant in the right place for her customers so that the new purchase will survive with a minimum of care and investment and not go to waste.

CHAPTER 4

What's the Location?

MANY GARDENS DON'T come to us as blank slates. They aren't always pristine rectangular lots with no issues of exposure, slope, sunlight, or wildlife. Usually, we inherit a series of limitations when we start to garden—whether they be from deer, brutal winds, or a dark grove of Norway maples. Often the most special locations are dramatic and intriguing because of these sorts of circumstances. I love being next to a huge shaded woodland of beech, hemlock, and ferns, but I resent the ravenous deer with their wide, innocent eyes, and I long for more sunlight so that I could have a proper vegetable garden. We gardeners like to push the envelope as much as nature will let us. The following gardens tell of people who have wanted to garden in often amazing, but restrictive, spots and succeeded by working with their site instead of against it—and that's a lesson for any homeowner even in the most homogenous suburb.

By the Sea

The idea of a coastal flower garden and up-to-date sustainability don't always match up. At Coleman and Susan Burke's seaside Nantucket house, traditional elements and lots of time-honored structural elements—clipped hedges, stone walls, wrought-iron gates, and a stately pergola—tie the garden to another, perhaps more gracious, era. But look closer. This garden contains ideas that move the concepts of water usage, native plantings, and conservation subtly forward in ways that benefit both the homeowner and the delicate surrounding wetland and maritime environment.

Coleman and Susan Burke's property sits in a magical spot on a narrow strip of land with Nantucket Harbor on one side and a grassy tidal salt marsh on the other. But as any seaside gardener will tell you, that doesn't make it an easy place to garden successfully.

Susan Burke, who began the garden in the mid-1990s, says these days her favorite part of her yard is not the most obvious—the glorious beachside plantings. Those beds are filled with a cottagey blend of poppies, mallows, beach roses,

Russian sage, and catmint that harkens back to *An Island Garden*, Celia Thaxter's famous 19th-century book about her flower plot on Appledore Island, Maine. Instead, in some ways Burke prefers the edges of her property: a subtle native garden on the other side of the house, with its green-on-green tones and twisted trunks of the salt-tolerant native beach plum (*Prunus maritima*) that make a romantically undomesticated transition to the beach and grassy tidal marshes.

Right from the beginning, she knew that to have any sort of garden so close to the ocean, she would have to protect her plantings from the drying winds and leaf desiccation from the salt spray, her main enemy. So she asked her friend George Schoellkopf, who owns Hollister House, a formal garden in Washington, Connecticut, to visit and advise her on creating a suitable barrier. After the first night of his visit, Schoellkopf casually presented her with a small sketch on a piece of notepaper that showed two straight lines ending in a circle. He had decided that what she needed was a ha-ha (the two lines) that runs parallel to the wide, columned porch of her house.

A long axis runs from the graveled herb garden down into a sunken stone ha-ha and then back up to a vine-covered arbor. Susan Burke, *above left*, can't walk through the garden without stopping to deadhead spent flowers and root out weeds every few steps.

Defined as "a fence, wall, etc., set in a ditch around a garden or park so as not to hide the view from within," the ha-ha was traditionally used in historic British gardens to keep livestock from the fields out of the lawn near the house. Here in Nantucket, the ha-ha idea has worked brilliantly and lives up to a name that derives from an 18th-century English gentleman's exclamation of discovery. The trench that Schoellkopf conceived is up to 7 feet deep and offers a garden surprise when seen from above. In fact, you can't fully appreciate this unexpected feature until you walk down into the garden and view it from either end. The ha-ha is lined with stone in irregular shapes and sizes, with seemingly random gaps left for planting. But as with most parts of this garden, those planting pockets are not really random. Over the years, Burke has pried up even more of the stones to create additional planting areas for a growing collection of filipendula,

Fairly fragile flowers like poppies are sheltered by a band of tough beach roses and shrubs and a sunken trench garden lined with stonework, *above and opposite below. Opposite top:* The front side of the Burkes' house looks out over a protected marsh.

hostas, astilbe, and cimicifuga. These perennials, in most situations pretty tough customers, would never thrive outside of the little bunker that shelters them from the wind and retains valuable moisture between its mossy rocks and soil.

On the far side of the ha-ha, there is a perennial walk of stepping-stones carpeted in thyme and lined with a rowdy mixture of native and nonnative pollinator-attracting plants that Burke's garden designer, Julie Jordin, helped her select. Butterfly weed (*Asclepias tuberosa*), joe-pye weed (*Eupatorium maculatum*), *Lavatera* 'Barnsley', purple ninebark (*Physocarpus opulifolius*), and huge balls of giant fleeceflower

(*Persicaria polymorpha*), which is not to be confused with the highly invasive knotweed (*Polygonum cuspidatum*) that it resembles, flourish just a few yards from the beachfront.

Even with such relatively intricate garden plantings, Burke's property is distinguished more by what goes on around its edges than what happens in the flower garden. She strives to keep the boundaries purposefully blurry, without adding obtrusive walls or fences to fend off the deer and rabbits. The perennial garden blends in seamlessly with a wind-blocking seaside barrier of natives: pepperbush (*Clethra alnifolia*), swamp mallows (*Hibiscus moscheutos*), and junipers. On the wetlands side is a stand of one of Burke's favorite plants, the groundsel tree or salt marsh elder (*Baccharis halimifolia*), interplanted with other coastal species. Burke keeps the grandchild-friendly lawn area to a minimum.

Antique stone objects, pavers, and garden ornaments, *above*, accent the wildness of the plantings, especially around the garden's edges. A millstone plumbed as a fountain weeps into a lily pond on one of two small areas of lawn on the property, *opposite bottom*.

The soft boundaries where the garden segues into its surrounding wilder areas are especially important to Burke, who remembers her New England grandmother's early admiration of native plants and the habitat sensitivity of Rachel Carson, author of *Silent Spring*.

Except for the damage caused by the occasional Nor'easter or even the rare hurricane, the garden is finished and—considering the amount of bloom it features—fairly worry-free. Increasingly influenced by the naturalistic perennial plantings of some of her favorite garden designers, Burke today finds herself considering a wilder array of native grasses and shrubs. As time goes by, she doesn't require so many flowers, as much as she loves them. She says she has learned so much more in the Nantucket garden than she has in any of her previous gardens. Looking out over the sea or the quiet, verdant view of the marsh, it's easy to see why. Egrets, red-tailed hawks, and ospreys fish, hunt, and nest as they did well before the first European ship spied the island in 1602.

Environmental Restrictions

Every urban gardener knows that trying to garden in the city can be an exercise in limitations. Even though Caroline Ellis's Nantucket garden sits on an expansive hilltop meadow in the country, there are restrictions she must honor. The house and fenced garden were built on what was originally grassy pasture. When the original owners subdivided the property in the 1980s, they wisely installed a firm set of land-use covenants: The pasture must be kept pristine but for a small, very specific envelope in which each house and garden may be sited. The size of this usable envelope may not be altered nor its placement shifted. Since Ellis and her husband built their house in 1996, they have been happy to work within the delineated conservation space to make their garden. They hired local designer Lucinda Young, an expert in the area's plants, to better integrate their plantings within the wild site and to help maintain the meadow. Instead of bringing the meadow grasses right up to the house on all sides, Ellis and Young created a fenced formal garden that sits within a defined area surrounded by belt of tupelo and sassafras trees and a rough hedgerow of wildlife-sustaining northeastern native shrubs and plants like inkberry (*Ilex glabra*), hay-scented fern (*Dennstaedtia punctilobula*), and winterberry (*Ilex verticillata*).

Inside the enclosure, Ellis is in the process of reducing her garden's dependence on flowers for interest. She wants her garden to have more year-round appeal by increasing the number of evergreen species and adding more in the way of leafy green structure. This four-season aspect is important to Ellis and her husband, since they spend the winter on the island as well. There is purposely very little lawn, only a small mown strip near the front door that keeps the wildness at a bit of a distance. At the rear of the house, the garden floor consists of diagonally laid square bluestone pavers outlined with Belgian blocks that are intentionally set with gaps.

A few rangy flowering plants like gaura, liatris, and verbascum pop up underneath two arching tupelos that bring the feeling of the outside wildness into the garden. As a counterpoint to the views of the harbor and oak forest from the front of the house, there is more of an enclosed feeling in the back, where barriers like an arbor of clipped hornbeam shelter a wooden bench. Ellis says that even though the arbor looks labor intensive, it only requires clipping a couple of times a

year, as do the espaliered peaches and pears that line the fence around her gravel kitchen garden. To keep the fruit trees in top productive shape, Ellis merely clips any unwanted shoots from the espaliers as she strolls around the garden. Over the years, Ellis has simplified by reducing the variety of plants that she grows and choosing replacements that don't hog water, since that valuable commodity can be hard to retain in the island's porous, sandbarlike geography.

Caroline Ellis and her husband worked with local designer Lucinda Young to design a garden of formal elements, *above*, that is hidden from the surrounding meadow by a buffer of native shrubs. *Overleaf*: Inside the fenced part of Caroline Ellis's property is a formal but relaxed series of spaces, including a kitchen garden, *top left and right*, and a seating area of shrubs and stone pavers, *bottom right*. A narrow strip of mown grass, *bottom left*, separates the meadow from the front of the house where chickens roam.

Steep Lots

Judy Kameon's transformation of a client's precipitously sloped front yard in Los Angeles is unconventional in its use of masses of bold plants. Kameon, a longtime resident of the hilly neighborhoods around the Silver Lake district, is well versed in the unique challenges inherent in gardening on a steep grade. In fact, she and her designers at Elysian Landscapes have become the go-to talent for hillsides. Many of the neighboring properties feature conventional clipped shrubs, roses, flowerbeds, and lawns—even on such precariously tilted sites. You have to pity the poor mower and wonder who, if anybody, actually uses those vertiginous yards. Kameon long ago jettisoned the notion that a front yard has to look like something leftover from a

Leave It to Beaver set. The irrigation needed for such outmoded plantings can erode the hillside, especially in geographically unstable areas like California, where months of dryness are often followed by torrential rains and mud slides. Kameon favors Mediterranean species of plants that thrive in the weather patterns and arid climate of Southern California and knit together a soil-stabilizing network of roots. The idea is not to create a garden that never needs water, but to create a planting that gets supplemental irrigation for the first few years and then is weaned down to rely less and less on added moisture.

Here the plant heights are varied to make the slope more interesting. Low groundcover rosemary and African

daisies mound around clumps of aloes, agaves, and shrubby perennials like echium, phormium, euphorbia, and Mexican sage, with barely an empty spot in sight (though a large echium did take a fatal tumble right before my visit). The various species form a carpet—or, more aptly, a wall tapestry—of brilliant silvers, blues, and browns that catches the backlit sun in ever-changing ways.

In Los Angeles, designer Judy Kameon planted this steep front-yard slope with a dense blanket of Mediterranean-climate species such as phormium, aloe, rosemary, artemisia, and grevillea that helps hold the soil in place, especially during storms. Unlike many inclined yards on the block, it doesn't require mowing.

Alien Invaders

Pampas grass (especially the species *Cortaderia jubata*) has a terrible reputation as a self-seeding noxious weed in parts of the western United States and Hawaii. However, landscape designer Judy Kameon values the plant for its dramatic stature and toughness in the face of drought, so she chose a sterile dwarf selection (*Cortaderia selloana* 'Pumila') and swears that she has never seen it self-seed in over a decade of using it in clients' gardens. To be extracautious, she refrains from planting it near the meadow areas around the hills of Malibu and Mulholland Drive. Some plants that are well behaved in one sort of garden can become invasive and go out of bounds if planted in the wrong place—and all bets may be off in years to come as the climate changes. As an example of the complicated issue of nonnative plants and invasiveness, she mentions several other useful plants that fall into similarly dicey territory, though they are near and dear to Angeleno gardeners. For example, certain plants not native to California—Mexican feather grass (*Nassella tenuissima*), some varieties of fountain grass, and euphorbia—can become problematic in this region if given the right (or, in this case, wrong) conditions near areas into which they might escape. It is hard to make a blanket statement about their use, since conditions vary so much from location to location. But as with any imported species, care should be taken when placing these plants, since they can invade wild or sensitive wetland areas when wind, water, or animals spread the seed.

Instead of planting the normal clipped hedge, Judy Kameon screened a circular driveway and front entrance of a house on a busy street in Los Angeles with large agaves and grasses, *above and opposite.*

On a Busy Street

At another house set on a busy street that gets more than its share of traffic, Kameon took out the ordinary lawn-filled front yard and planted tall waving stands of ornamental grasses, phormium, and sculptural cactus in shades of jade green, silver blue, and brown around the half-circle driveway. Even though she wanted to give her clients a feeling of privacy from the street, Kameon felt that it would be a mistake to enclose the property with a fortresslike hedge or wall. Instead, she made a screen of large, loosely grouped plants to establish some separation while still addressing the street and neighborhood in an engaging way. One of the yard's most dominant plants has been controversial in recent years, and not just because—for some trendier souls—pampas grass is hopelessly out of style due to its overuse in mid-20th-century suburban plantings. But here in this garden, the plant's feathery seed heads and razor-thin leaves look almost primordial when surrounded by giant agaves, aloes, and groundcovers of asparagus fern and senecio.

Planting Deerproof Bulbs in the Lawn

At my own upstate lake cabin in Sullivan County, New York, my partner and I have been gardening for several years now. We deal with hungry deer from every side, so we're always testing what they will allow us to grow. One of the most successful steps we've taken is to turn our front lawn into a meadow of spring bulbs. Every fall, we add a few more varieties to the turf. April through May, it's a beautiful sight when thousands of daffodils, irises, snowdrops, crocus, camassias, squills, and glory-of-the-snow poke through the turf to make something that looks like a medieval unicorn tapestry. We avoid tulips, since they would get chomped off as soon as they bloom.

- Plant the bulbs in groups by digging fairly large half-moon slices out of the turf and pulling back the sod layer like a piece of carpet.

- Each hole gets a multitiered arrangement of large and small bulbs that will bloom over a period of 6 weeks or so. Follow the listed planting depth instructions for each variety.

- Add some bulb food. Refill the hole, water the bulbs, and lightly tamp down the "lid" of sod with your foot.

It's a hard autumn day's work to get all the planting done, but all the effort is very much worth it in the spring when the first shoots come out of the ground, lifting bits of dead leaves on the stalks as they grow. Over time, the bulbs will naturalize if they are happy and get enough sun, but I can't help but order more each year.

Small rock garden bulbs such as *Iris histrioides* 'Katharine Hodgkin,' *above*, and *Iris danfordiae*, *below*, succeed in our yard where deer-tempters like tulips never will.

Every fall I say I won't add any more bulbs to the front lawn of our upstate lake cabin, *above*, but every year I do so anyway. Most *Narcissus* 'Pistachio', *below right*, and *Scilla siberica*, *below left*, come back year after year, but some varieties only make a single grand performance.

Rooftop Gardening

As space gets tighter and tighter in our cities, more people are looking skyward for patches to cultivate. The tops of buildings in cities like New York and Chicago used to be barren. It is hard to imagine today that anyone would have wasted such important real estate—but they did and still do. When I first moved into my old apartment on 19th Street in Manhattan in 1989, the previous tenants, a young actress and two male models, had done nothing with the rooftop, even though there was a sliding glass door out from the bedroom and an outdoor faucet for a hose. Maybe my social life wasn't as demanding as theirs, but I wasn't going to let that valuable area go unused. That windy spot is where I learned to garden, and I still admire people who insist on gardening precariously several stories above the street.

Two such people, Chris and Lisa Goode, are rapidly making a name for themselves in the expanding world of New York City roof gardens (green roofs, in particular). As they developed a garden design business, Goode Green, the husband-and-wife team have learned by doing, especially as they investigated the technology needed to make a green roof on top of a commercial building that they own in New York's Little Italy. The two-level garden is like an elevated slice of the country, with a small lawn for their young daughter, egg-laying chickens, a kitchen garden, and a green roof meadow of wildflowers on top of the penthouse. Raised planting beds surround the 5- to 8-inch-deep lawn bed, which functions to cool the building and mitigate heat in the summertime. Layers of liner and green roof fabrics under the planted surface help reduce the amount of water that the plantings need. Any excess water from the planters goes right into the lawn; Goode says the topic of lawns just doesn't have the same negative connotation for her since she almost never has to directly irrigate her rooftop version.

Chris and Lisa Goode's New York City rooftop gravel kitchen garden is packed with vegetables, herbs, fruit trees, and berries watered with collected rainwater, whenever possible.

Each area of the Goodes' large roof garden has a distinct character: a loose meadow of sedums and wildflowers on the top of the penthouse, *above and below*; a strictly modern front-door water feature, *opposite top*; and a small lawn surrounding raised beds and formal clipped screens of hornbeams, *opposite below*.

On the other side of the penthouse, there is a kitchen garden of raised beds set on gravel that gives the family the enviable ability to pick berries (5 gallons alone last summer) for breakfast as well as herbs, lettuce, and vegetables for dinner. This garden is partly watered with rainwater captured from the roof through downspouts channeled into a galvanized metal cistern. Looking down on all of this is a seed-sown rooftop meadow where butterfly weed, coreopsis, poppies, and echinacea thrive surrounded by a mat of sedum. The unexpected planting, which receives no irrigation other than rain, is frequently visited by butterflies, birds, and insects when it is in bloom.

Rooftop gardens aren't a weekend project. They need a lot of planning, and the setup costs can obviously be high since you are importing soil and a garden where there would be none otherwise. Most of the plants and building materials of this garden had to be hoisted up to the sixth floor roof with cranes. Weight is the other big consideration and requires the

Amy Falder, *opposite*, and Chris Brunner installed a lushly planted green roof meadow on top of carriage house behind a client's brownstone.

A Rooftop Meadow in Brooklyn

Butterfly milkweed (*Asclepias tuberosa*)

Showy aster (*Aster spectabilis* or *Eurybia spectabilis*)

Blue false indigo (*Baptisia australis*)

Yellow coneflower (*Echinacea paradoxa*)

Blazing star (*Liatris scariosa* var. *novae-angliae*)

Bitter switchgrass (*Panicum amarum*)

Little bluestem (*Schizachyrium scoparium*)

White stonecrop (*Sedum album*)

Kamschatca stonecrop (*Sedum kamtschaticum*)

Watch-chain stonecrop (*Sedum sexangulare*)

Dwarf goldenrod (*Solidago sphacelata* 'Golden Fleece')

Prairie dropseed (*Sporobolus heterolepis*)

Fameflower (*Talinum calycinum*)

expertise of an engineer to judge the roof's structural soundness. The overall plantable depth of the meadow, for example, is 4 inches, which works out to weigh about 25 pounds per square foot when saturated. All the while, of course, the drainage system has to be in top order. But the secret to any successful green roof is the quality of the specific components, which can change depending on the site conditions. Goode describes a sort of layer cake: a membrane appropriate for green roofs, a root barrier if needed, a separation fabric, drainage mats, and filter fabrics that wick the water to cups that retain the moisture so that it can be used by the plants.

The Goodes are not alone in remaking New York City's skyline. Amy Falder and Chris Brunner of New York Green Roofs design and install planted surfaces to deal with issues of storm-water runoff, heat reduction, and energy conservation. They have designed nearly 40 projects around the city, ranging from 2-inch-deep fields of succulents for the roofs of office buildings and university dorms to a 6-inch-deep flowering meadow garden on top of a Brooklyn carriage house. For the latter type of project, Falder says that first it's most important to know the weight restrictions of the building from an engineers' report. This determines the soil profile and possible depth and the most suitable plant palette for the situation. A deep layer of up to 10 to 12 inches of soil will sustain perennials, grasses, and even shallow-rooted shrubs, while a thinner 1½-inch layer would sustain only low-growing sedums. The designers like to use primarily North American native plants that will thrive on a city roof with a minimum of added water—though certain imported sedum species are too important to green roof gardening to resist. A roof made of just drought-tolerant sedums doesn't usually require supplemental irrigation, but perennials and grasses will need water if the weather is dry.

Consider the Materials

PART II

CHAPTER 5

Gravel Takes Center Stage

STYLISTICALLY, GRAVEL BRINGS a wealth of visual allusions to a garden. It evokes the modernist desert cactus plantings of Palm Springs, the sophisticated shady dining terraces of Provence, or the old walled herb garden of an estate in England. Gravel doesn't have to be a poor substitute for people who can't or don't want to have a lawn. More and more landscape designers are taking advantage of the material's reductive quality as a blank canvas to accentuate unusual plant specimens and architectural features. Even purposefully shaggy beds full of disparate varieties of wild-looking plants seem tidier when surrounded by gravel paths. On the other hand, a garden of pared-down, restrained elements and a limited plant palette can make a gravel garden poetically minimal and exceptionally modern.

Reflooring the Garden

On the street where I grew up in Abilene, Texas, there was only one lawnless front yard, and it was made mostly of gravel. The older woman who lived there—we neighborhood kids called her the Gravel Lady—was one of a handful of home-owners on the street who actively gardened instead of just maintained her yard. Under tall mesquite trees, she grew drought-tolerant plants like yuccas, agaves, and santolina that no one else seemed to want to grow, though these species were obviously well-suited to our West Texas climate. Her unconventional garden convinced all the neighborhood kids

A front garden in Austin, Texas, designed by Dylan Robertson uses a mixture of pavers and crushed stone planted with trees, shrubs, cacti, and groundcovers chosen for their sculptural shapes. The reduced amount of lawn is elevated in a carbon steel frame.

that the Gravel Lady was a bona fide witch—and we gave her house a wide berth. In my secret heart of hearts, however, I was fascinated by the Gravel Lady's garden. I often snuck down the block to shyly admire her spare style of planting and the understated beauty of her gravel, each stone a slightly different shade from the others. I remember the sight of dozens of wonderfully

delicate *Anemone coronaria* poking up out of the stones, surrounded by huge blue agaves and flat pads of purple sand verbena. I love that remembered image; now, all these years later, I still reference it when I see gravel used well in a garden.

At a house in Austin, Texas, landscape designer Dylan Robertson of D-Crain Design and Construction took a traditional front yard that normally would have been a bland, flat expanse of turf and carved it into several distinctly modern areas that take the demands of the local climate in stride. Austin gardens have two relatively bare seasons. One is a mild winter, where snow is uncommon but temperatures can fall into the twenties. The other comes with the long, blazingly hot summers that force humans and plants alike to sulk until autumn comes. Here, plants and the surfaces that surround them need to be carefully selected so that they look good year-round and manage to withstand the summer ordeal. To address this quandary, Robertson avoided seasonal planting of swapped-out bedding plants in favor of a design that would hold its own all year.

To soften the sharp, modern edges of the house and garden design, Robertson used statuesque plants that have a graphic quality, such as *Agave weberi,* shoestring acacia (*Acacia stenophylla*), Mexican weeping bamboo (*Otatea acuminata*), and asparagus fern. He knit these different shapes together in their crushed limestone gravel beds with carpets of drought-resistant groundcovers and flowering thyme. Three clipped boxwood balls add an unexpected bit of old-school tradition that comes off as appealingly quirky in the otherwise stripped-down setting. There is also a nod to the traditional front-yard lawn, but in this case it has been elevated and framed with a low retaining wall of carbon steel. Set off in this way, a patch of ordinary turf becomes a sculptural object in the design of the garden rather than a space-filling background.

At another unusual front yard designed by Robertson in West Austin, several species of agave, including colorfully striped versions of *Agave americana* (both blue forms and thread-leaf varieties), provide a strong backbone to wispy plants such as Mexican feather grass (*Nassella tenuissima*),

Mats of thyme and succulents mingle with tufts of asparagus fern and Mexican weeping bamboo to cushion the crisp edges of this design in Austin, Texas.

here in the northern part of its native territory, and colorful wildflowers like coreopsis. Evergreen 'Winter Gem' box-wood and shrubby rosemary loosely dot a front yard of crushed limestone and pavers that leads off of a circular driveway. There isn't a front lawn in sight. Instead, Robertson gave this space a lush green feeling by layering a complex variety of heights of grasses, cacti, shrubs, and small trees around the front of the property. This staggered design is echoed by a planted walkway of raised weathered-steel cube planters in the forecourt that dramatically display agaves, grasses, and silver ponyfoot (*Dichondra argentea*), a gracefully flowing Texas native, as you walk in from the street.

Above: Ordinarily, this front yard in Austin, Texas, might feature a prim, house-hugging foundation planting of evergreens and flowerbeds surrounded by green turf. Dylan Robertson takes a looser, more water-conscious approach with a mixture of agaves, boxwood, and wispy stands of Mexican feather grass surrounded by crushed stone and pavers. *Opposite:* Dan Seaver and Will Speck found only bare earth, straggly rose bushes, and an old toilet in the front yard when they bought their house in Venice, California. Working with their landscape architect, Mark Tessier, they added a raised wooden boardwalk that leads from the gate to the front door, passing over a newly graveled area planted with grasses, phormium, and kangaroo paws. Instead of a ratty lawn, there is now a patchwork of low succulents, *opposite bottom,* that knits the sleek new design together.

How to Lay Down Gravel

- Each site is different, so first determine the grade and elevation of the area. This will determine how much soil will have to be removed to level the gravel with surrounding features, like a sidewalk. As a guide, a simple level site might need to have 2 to 2½ inches of soil taken away to be used elsewhere.

- The underlying soil should be flat and fairly dense. If it is soft and loose, use (or hire someone to use) a plate compactor machine.

- Landscape architect Christy Ten Eyck recommends putting down only ½ to 1 inch of gravel on top of road base (the compacted crushed limestone that's used for highways). A deeper layer of gravel can be a chore to trudge through.

- Some gardeners like to use a permeable black filter cloth under their gravel to keep weeds from sprouting while letting air and water through. Though you won't have weeds, the gravel tends to migrate. Over time you may need to apply extra stones on top to keep the black cloth from showing.

- Gravel is sold in different grades or sizes such as ⅜ inch or ¾ inch. Consider using a mixture of two or three sizes so that the voids between the stones will be smaller. This way, the gravel will give less under your feet and be easier to walk on.

- Expect to top off your gravel with a couple of bags every few years to fill blank patches.

Ten Eyck and her husband, Gary Deaver, relax a moment under the impressive live oaks that create a cool roof over the gravel areas near the front of their house.

Softening the Hardscape

There is a line between a successful (i.e., comfortable) gravel garden and one that feels like the homeowner has been handed down a harsh punishment. A range of plant textures and colors will help cushion the harsh visual blow of a garden made predominantly of stone. Los Angeles landscape designer Jay Griffith remembers a drought that hit the city when he first started his business in 1974, sending homeowners scrambling to pave or gravel over their lawns indiscriminately. In some circumstances, the trend was to get out the concrete mixer and rashly cover over almost all signs of bare earth (the designer claims that he has noticed a correlation between retired men of a certain age and cement mixers). Griffith encountered this kind of expansive use of concrete at a double lot he was hired to redesign for architect Tom Carson and filmmaker Nicole Bettauer, the home's new owners. Griffith knew his first task was to break up the hard, impermeable surface that had been mainly used as a parking lot between several outbuildings. As is his usual custom, he wanted to avoid hauling the heavy pieces off-site. Armed with a diamond blade saw, his crew cut many of the slabs into square pavers and lined them up to form more permeable paths through beds of coarse gravel. Other slabs were stacked up to make "banquettes" covered with cushions for lounging around—something of a signature for the designer. "I always try to imagine myself in the spaces I design," Griffith says, and since he claims to be happiest lying down, his gardens often include an outdoor daybed or two.

Designer Jay Griffith frames the seating areas of the Carson Bettauer backyard in Venice, California, with big stands of blue green *Agave attenuata*, striped aeonium, Mexican blue palm (*Brahea armata*), and oxblood red *Euphorbia cotinifolia*. The planted screens segregate what would otherwise be one open space and set up a soft structural division that contrasts nicely with the hard edges of the pavers.

Jay Griffith's gardens exhibit a refined color palette that depends on leaves more than flowers and a talent for framing interior views and outdoor seating areas.

He combined these aesthetic concerns with a desire to conserve resources like water and building materials long before it was fashionable.

Griffith, whose design projects range from small Venice backyards for friends to huge Malibu estates for celebrity clients, has a talent for creating distinctively modern plant combinations that has helped him redefine the planting palette all over his hometown and create a Los Angeles look (e.g., sophisticated plants set off by serene expanses of pavers and crushed stone). The style replaced a more higgledy-piggledy mix of imported species and architecture from Spanish to Tudor. He attributes his skill and success to influences of his own: several female landscape designers and architects with whom he came up through the ranks in the early days of his career. Though the garden design scene in Los Angeles at that period was what he refers to as "a man's game," he found himself drawn more to the environmental sensitivity of California designers like Isabelle Greene, Pamela Burton, and Nancy Goslee Power. Most important, he noticed the innovative things these designers were doing with a new palette of more regionally suitable plants from the different Mediterranean-type climate areas around the world, such as Chile, Australia, and South Africa. Though unusual at the time, these imported species would come to form the horticultural hallmark of many West Coast gardens from San Diego to Marin County over the next decades.

In other parts of California and the Southwest, ever-tighter restrictions on water usage and the corresponding need to scale back on irrigation have made the cultivation of a perfect lawn a near crime. South of San Francisco, Bernard Trainor, a local garden designer, also has become known for his extensive use of crushed stone. A native of Australia, Trainor is transforming his local Silicon Valley gardening landscape and the plants that populate it.

Long-blooming perennials like these red kangaroo paws keep going all summer.

Underneath a dramatically spreading oak, Bernard Trainor created a simple design in a side yard of a house in Menlo Park, California. From a local boulder plumbed as a fountain, water weeps out of a hole drilled in the top and circulates into a small reservoir concealed by gravel.

Opposite: At the same Menlo Park property, an awkward strip of yard runs behind the house next to the neighbor's fence. Instead of ignoring the space, as many homeowners would do, Trainor gave the clients his own version of a sculpture garden made of a series of head-high copper poles, each topped with a small river stone. The installation has an almost totemic appearance and an unexpected presence for all of its simplicity, almost as if the visitor were walking through a group of standing figures. *Above:* Nearby, Trainor designed a gravel backyard to the relatively small modernist house by Joseph Eichler to add space for entertaining and outdoor living.

At another one of his projects in Menlo Park, Trainor took what was once the house's front and side yards and refashioned them into a private, and infinitely more useful, walled gravel garden. Finding the space blessed with the dappled shade of an existing, beautifully branched California or coast live oak (*Quercus agrifolia*), Trainor knew he didn't have to do much except strive not to spoil it with overdesign.

He created an outdoor living room furnished with a dining table and a low stone wall that can be used as seating for larger parties—all under the serene "ceiling" of the twisted oak limbs. A few Mediterranean-climate plants, such as mountain flax (*Phormium cookianum*) and acanthus, add to the quiet emptiness of the space.

For the backyard of a midcentury house designed by Joseph Eichler, in Palo Alto, he made a dry garden worthy of a desert. This simple design may not seem revolutionary—until the property is seen in the context of its lushly irrigated neighborhood of shaded, tree-lined streets and conventional suburban plantings. Instead of trying to mimic or compete with the rectilinear lines of the house, he made a faux naturalistic installation that's not intended to fool anyone with its authenticity. The mix of Mexican agaves, reedlike restios such as cape rush (*Elegia tectorum* syn. *Chondropetalum tectorum*) from South Africa, Australian kangaroo paws (*Anigo-*

zanthos), and even the surprisingly drought-tolerant South African asparagus fern (*Asparagus densiflorus*) creates a garden that was clearly designed and not merely a misplaced patch of the Mojave.

Sean Knibb, a Los Angeles–based landscape designer, is known for the lavish gardens he creates for Hollywood clients, but recently he devised an affordably priced modular gravel garden that can be adapted to any flat site of 750 to 3,000 square feet. Remarkably, it is sold and installed by the foot, like carpet. Sound like a gimmick? Well, maybe it is to a degree, but it's not a cynical one. Knibb says his main goal was to give people who wouldn't normally be able to afford his services access to a stylish, water-wise garden that goes beyond the everyday fare of cacti and succulents.

Modularity aside, the display garden that Knibb created for this new concept at his showroom on a hip stretch of Abbot Kinney in Venice is gracefully simple on its own merits. In it, he emphasizes plants with a sense of tradition and sets them off with a "floor" of rough crushed stone in a larger size than is normally seen. A backdrop of boxwood and a screening hedge of ficus contain dark, dusky-colored roses, waving *Verbena bonariensis,* and gaura. A mixture of native grasses, imported Mediterranean species like African daisy (*Arctotis*), and edible artichokes, strawberries, fava beans, and herbs surround the perimeter.

Behind his Venice, California, studio, Sean Knibb, *below*, has created a showcase for a low-water modular garden that is sold by the yard, thus saving the cost of his custom design fees.

A Permeable Surface

It's not only in a hot, dry climate, however, that gravel makes a popular alternative to lawn. In rainy areas such as the East Coast or the Pacific Northwest, a layer of small stones creates an elegant unifying—and porous—garden layer. In contrast to concrete slabs, its open composition allows excess water to percolate easily through the small stones down into the soil. The permeability issue is near and dear to environmentally conscious landscape and garden makers around the world. The small stones also perform a function similar to common wood-chip mulch: retaining soil moisture during drier periods and holding water and soil in place during downpours.

Elements of this lawn-free, highly permeable approach are stylishly executed in the garden of Carin Goldberg and Jim Biber in the Carroll Gardens section of Brooklyn. When the couple moved in, the long and narrow backyard was fairly typical for the borough, with its dilapidated, mismatched fence of green plastic and chain link surrounding a sad patch of weedy lawn. Aside from a stone patio furnished with tables and chairs, the sunny yard was not used very much. The couple—who both work in visual fields, she as a graphic designer and he as an architect—wanted something that reflected their graphic sensibilities but didn't require intensive gardening knowledge or maintenance. They hired garden designer Susan Welti of Foras Studio, who came up with an innovative solution, a plan of planted squares that would create a geometric backdrop to the patio and provide an interesting year-round view from every window on the rear of the house. Of course, a person can take a stroll (albeit a short one) around the yard or even do a little clipping or weeding if the spirit moves him. But this is primarily a viewing garden, much like a classical Japanese rock garden. As it's designed, the best view of the disciplined arrangement of squares is from the house.

This isn't a garden that would necessarily satisfy people who like to putter around tending plants, as many of us gardeners do. These plants are formalized elements in a strict design. Clipped boxwood, *Hydrangea macrophylla*, Solomon's seal (*Polygonatum odoratum* 'Variegatum'), Russian sage (*Perovskia atriplicifolia*), and Mexican feather grass (*Nassella tenuissima*) fill the squares in different degrees of looseness. The striking contrasts between the textures of the tight cushions of boxwood and the flowing stems of grasses and perennials keep this garden from looking too sterile. Some people have a problem when a garden's plantings become too spare and flowerless—I don't. Spare is just another flavor. This is a garden for those who love plants not so much for their horticulture but for the pure, simple beauty of their graphic forms.

Permeable garden materials are not just good options for dry climates. In a wetter spot like this New York City garden designed by Susan Welti, gravel easily handles sudden East Coast downpours.

Simplicity is an important goal as well for Yvonne Tocquigny in her garden in a historic neighborhood in Austin, Texas. The busy owner of a successful interactive marketing firm had previously lived in a house with an expansive ¾-acre lawn that required a great deal of yard work, including annoyingly noisy lawn mowing and maintenance. In 2002, Tocquigny wanted to scale down and bought and renovated a West Austin house that she enlarged and opened to the outdoors with large windows. Tocquigny specifically did not want a lawn. She worked with two separate garden designers, Berthold Haas and Patrick Kirwin, to come up with a contemplative garden of four square beds surrounding a central fountain that is reminiscent of examples in medieval monastery gardens. The space is reductive in style but far from stark. Its quiet restfulness seems entirely appropriate to Texas's often intense heat and humidity.

Underneath this calm surface, there was a lot of work to be done to make Tocquigny's new garden successful and thoughtfully connected to its surroundings. The designers and contractor laid down a layer of well-draining Texas caliche (a common type of local crushed limestone) for the Mediterranean-style plantings. A slight, visually imperceptible grade slanting toward the arroyo was engineered to direct excess storm water away from the house. The garden's distinctive stonework walls, planters, and fountain were built and carved from local limestone by Haas and his craftsmen. Coincidentally, Haas was trained by his sculptor father in the Black Forest region of Germany, known for limestone and springs much like the Hill Country around Austin. As he has segued into garden design, Haas still considers water a primary focus for the restful atmosphere it creates.

A limited palette of well-chosen plant species softens the stone surfaces. The grassy foliage of irises, mostly in yellow with a few purple interlopers, crowd the raised planters.

Previous page: Water drainage is a consideration in Yvonne Tocquigny's formally arranged but loosely planted garden in Austin. Storm water is directed over gravel and an underlayer of crushed limestone on its way to a small arroyo (dry creek) behind the property. In the rear garden, the doors of the back house slide open for dinner parties. *Above and opposite:* A doorway in the hedgelike trellis separates the main garden area with its splashing fountain and a narrow side area planted with herbs in Tocquigny's garden.

Around the planters' bases billow Lindheimer's fern (*Thelypteris normalis*), a sun-loving and drought-resistant native of the Texas roadside. Santa Barbara daisies (*Erigeron karvinskianus*) seed themselves and hold up well to foot traffic near spring-blooming bulbs like bicolored lady tulips (*Tulipa clusiana*) and prairie onion (*Allium textile*). A large, open metal trellis shades the back south-facing wall of the main house. It is covered with fragrant vines of Confederate jasmine (*Trachelospermum jasminoides*) that bloom exuberantly in springtime and periodically afterward.

Where Does Gravel Come From?

Pea gravel isn't a manufactured product. It's not even a renewable resource. The choice rounded pebbles are mined, most often from glacial deposits or banks of rivers and other bodies of water where they have gathered over millennia. This doesn't occur just anywhere, but in ancient spots where the conditions for alluvial accumulation are just right. To get to the buried material, an open pit mine is required. First, any trees and plants are removed, and then the topsoil is scraped away (this is reserved to be reused or replaced later). Once the gravel is extracted, it's graded for size and washed. Even with the required remediation, the environment of the particular mine will never be the same. For this reason and others, many environmentally conscious landscape designers have lately stopped specifying naturally smoothed pea gravel and also the popular, black Mexican beach pebbles (you'll see examples of both of the former in this book, but few gardens are beyond reproach, especially those that were constructed a number of years ago). Forward-thinking designers are switching to more jagged, crushed limestone or granite instead. Crushed stone is literally that, broken-up pieces of mined stone. These quarries are also an environmental disturbance, but since there is more whole stone to be crushed in the world than there is pea gravel to be mined, allowances are made.The mining of all aggregates (which includes sand) is destructive to the landscape when the pits are opened and the contents are washed, sifted, and graded. Responsible companies are required to remediate these

quarries once they are exhausted. Some are replanted to approximate their original condition, while others are turned into reservoirs. Crushed stone is a heavy but an inexpensive commodity, so chances are it hasn't traveled far. And the gardening sector of the gravel market is tiny compared to its use in construction and highway building, but nonetheless we should still pay attention and encourage our local suppliers to answer the tough environmental questions. When purchasing from some of the big chain stores, it may be hard to figure out how the supply system is working, since they seem to have similar gravel brands nationwide. It's another reason to support your local nursery. As with so many environmental choices, the decisions we make trying to do the right thing are complex and often somewhat overwhelming.

When choosing the materials for a gravel garden, consider whether the material is locally mined crushed stone, *opposite*, or naturally smoothed pebble dug out of glacial deposits, *above*.

CHAPTER 6
Stone and Steel

NOT EVERY WATER-CONSCIOUS garden maker can—or wants to—rely only on gravel or crushed stone to increase permeability. Some people don't care for the rough crunch of gravel under their feet, nor do they like they way the pebbles tend to scratch up the floor when tracked indoors. I love the evocative sound of footsteps on gravel. For those who prefer a more solid surface, concrete or stone pavers interspersed with plants or smaller amounts of gravel make better alternatives than asphalt and solid slabs of concrete or brick butted edge to edge. These impermeable surfaces only aggravate sudden flooding, allowing no place for the rush of water to go as it follows gravity in search of a drain.

Even tough, enduring building materials like carbon steel, *opposite,* or stone pavers, *above,* can be recycled or reused.

Keeping It Local

I remember scouting an estate in the Bay Area several years ago for a magazine. While we toured the property, the garden designer explained that the stone for his client's imposing hillside terraces had been rescued from villages and archaeological sites in China that were threatened by the building of the Three Gorges Dam on the Yangtze River. Rescuing stone that would have been lost under hundreds of feet of water sounds admirable and almost noble, but beautiful as the terrace was, all I could think about was the huge amount of money, fuel, and energy it took to lug those heavy stones from their remote valley. Deeming such long-distance importation of materials as a "rescue" appears misguided as well, since it seems to me that

The Immobile Beauty of Pavers

Stone slabs can be expensive, but they are enduring, and, unlike gravel, they don't need to be replenished as the years go by. For a garden in the Noe Valley neighborhood of San Francisco, James Lord and Roderick Wyllie of Surface Design wanted to make a stylish, low-maintenance space for their hardworking clients. The central feature of the 25- by 50-foot yard is a sleek terrace that can be used for parties. Instead of butting the entire pattern of diagonal stone pieces, gaps were left and planted with graphic green lines of mondo grass (*Ophiopogon japonicus*). The gaps easily allow water to drain between the stones, and the mondo grass is walkable. On either side of the terrace, green-on-green beds of Corsican hellebores (*Helleborus argutifolius*), Japanese boxwood (*Buxus microphylla japonica*), button fern (*Pellaea rotundifolia*), and weaver's bamboo (*Bambusa textilis*) remain bright all year long—a necessity in the Bay Area's mild climate, where outdoor spaces can be enjoyed in four seasons. A tall wooden fence encloses the space for privacy's sake; two sides of the fence are painted an unexpected ebony black.

Even in such a simple garden design, challenges can arise from unexpected places. When the client wanted to include a spa, Lord and Wyllie had to devise a way to incorporate the large functional object in the middle of the spare design. To make it unobtrusive, the designers installed a moveable wooden platform on rails that can be rolled easily back and forth over the pavers to uncover the spa. When pushed farther down the garden, the platform serves as a table for parties. The garden's convertible nature is a good example of how clever design can accomplish a lot in a small space—similar to a Murphy bed in a New York City apartment.

Not too many blocks away in San Francisco, designer Beth Mullins of Growsgreen Landscape Design constructed

a truly philanthropic endeavor would extract the stone and use it to rebuild the soon-to-be-destroyed homes of the villagers elsewhere.

The food movement prides itself on the use of local materials, and the same use should be commended in the garden. I propose that we keep stone pretty much in the region where it was quarried. In the present economy, it seems outdated to brag about an exotic material that has been imported from the most difficult or remote source. In addition, local stone is often the best choice for the sake of visual suitability. What looks more natural in a landscape than native stone that matches the color and tone of the soil around it?

Above and opposite: In a San Francisco garden designed by Roderick Wyllie and James Lord, a wooden deck rolls on metal tracks to hide an unsightly spa. The stone pavers are set in an open pattern to absorb rainfall.

Below: There's no lawn mower needed in a backyard of pavers and groundcovers designed by Beth Mullins in San Francisco, just some clipping several times a year to keep the groundcover in bounds.

a garden that also incorporates stone in an innovative way. The owner of the moist, shady backyard in the Haight wanted to have a garden that would look attractive all year, especially from the rear windows of the row house. Plus she didn't want to mow. Mullins planted tiny-leaved baby's tears (*Soleirolia soleirolii*) that creeps between the locally sourced granite curbs. Even though the groundcover is not specifically drought tolerant, it does well in the garden's shady situation and frequent fog of that section of the city. Every few months as it starts to cover the stones, Mullins cuts the baby's tears back to keep it looking tidy.

In a narrow garden in Austin, Texas, Margot Thomas worked with landscape architect James David to come up with a lawn-free solution to liven up a heavily shaded front yard and a small backyard linked by a narrow side walkway. In front, where the shade of a dense southern magnolia made the yard inhospitable to regular turf, the area had already been planted with mondo grass. David removed a stepping-stone path and consolidated the walkway into one large terrace made of Austin brick that Thomas already had on-site. Called "common" bricks because of their rough edges, these structural building materials were historically intended to be hidden behind a cladding of more refined "face" brick. But David loved their rustic look and kept them in the foreground. To give the front yard more interest, David interspersed the brick with irregularly shaped bluestone pavers and added a modern concrete square fountain that anchors the corner of the property, extending the soothing sound of water to both screened porch and sidewalk. The backyard patio, with its bent metal cafe chairs and trestle table, is undeniably reminiscent of New Orleans, the hometown that both David and Thomas share. At the owner's request, David did not alter the backyard's existing sultry subtropical plantings of palmetto, cycad, and the more water-intensive ornamental ginger (which though heat loving, can be problematic during periods of drought).

Opposite and below: Lawn would never thrive beneath the dense shade of a tall magnolia tree in Margot Thomas's Austin, Texas, yard. James David replaced it with groundcovers, stone, and salvaged brick anchored by a sleekly modern fountain.

On a steeply sloped backyard in San Francisco, James Lord and Roderick Wyllie constructed imposing planters of carbon steel and filled them with perennials like penstemons, campanulas, and Japanese anemones. The ramped and stepped pathways lead down to a small lawn that absorbs runoff.

Carbon Steel

Though the initial costs would be high, long-lasting metal infrastructure can rescue a site that otherwise might be unusable and eroded. By making planters and terraces buttressed with weathered carbon steel, James Lord and Roderick Wyllie of Surface Design transformed an exceedingly narrow hillside backyard that was blessed with amazing views of San Francisco and the bay but was too steep to be useful. The clients wanted to enjoy the area in several different ways—including the incorporation of a small lawn. Lord and Wyllie knit the slope together with paneled angular boxes of the recyclable steel, which by design oxidizes and forms its own protective coat of rust. Sometimes the boxes act as walls to define a stepped gravel walk; in other sections, they become raised planters for cascading flowering plants. The long-lasting untreated steel follows the lines of preexisting mid-century walls left from the previous owners. Gravel-filled runnels absorb some of the extra rainwater, and the rest is directed down alongside the walkways toward the lawn.

Thwarting the Landfill

Sometimes a surfeit of stone can be a problem. The effort and expense of hauling refuse containers full of unwanted debris from the dismantling of an existing city garden are real issues for most homeowners, especially when people are so often confronted by a forgotten area full of weeds and small boulders. While renovating the backyard of a historic Harlem brownstone for Paul and Susan Huck, garden designers Emma de Caires and Nathaniel Harris of Blue Dahlia Gardens came upon a large amount of glacially smoothed stones that would have been too heavy and too expensive to remove. Such space-hogging but ultimately useful things needn't be relegated to a landfill, a fact that isn't always apparent to designers. Luckily, the rounded stones are beautiful enough to keep on-site and use as building materials. In fact, no stone was removed for this particular project. Instead, they now edge flowerbeds filled with a variety of plants, including native cardinal flower (*Lobelia cardinalis*), liatris, and echinacea. They also outline paths of dark bluestone aggregate. More of these on-site stones—along with some decorative stones bought from a supplier—were used to make an unusual alternative to ordinary lawn and as a base for a quirky assemblage of found objects and a bubbling fountain.

Opposite top and bottom: Where previously there was just an eroded, muddy slope, garden terraces now create flat, useful spaces simply furnished with gravel in San Francisco. Above: Faced with garden soil littered with hundreds of rounded stones, Emma de Caires and Nathaniel Harris gathered the heavy foundlings to create borders and beds in Paul and Susan Huck's Harlem backyard.

CHAPTER 7

The Intentional Lawn

WITH ALL THIS talk of gravel and stone, please don't think I'm entirely antilawn. There is a great need for cool, green surfaces in our cities and suburbs, and grassy areas are certainly a better surface than acres of asphalt and impermeable concrete. These heat diffusers, however, don't necessarily need to be made of traditional turf. Americans have unquestioningly carried our favorite lawn—the nonnative, water-loving Kentucky bluegrass (*Poa pratensis*)—to all parts of the wilderness that we've developed over the past several hundred years. If you live in the cooler, wetter Northeast, then such a shallow-rooted grass might succeed without too much effort. But if you transplant that green carpet to drought-stricken places like Southern California, you're asking for real difficulties.

Rethinking Turf

The move to rethink our use of grassy lawns is nothing new. I'd like to echo the chorus of people who are urging those gardeners who haven't made the change to alter how they think about conventional turf, no matter where they live. If you would like to keep a lawn—perhaps for the kids, perhaps just because you like the look of it—then reduce it to a smaller area that is intentional and purposeful. Too often, we use sod as a default surface, as if we were coloring in the empty spaces between our houses, driveways, and flowerbeds with a giant green felt-tip marker. We can all strive to make the design of our yards more informed by the future rather than merely mimicking the inherited attitudes and lawn-heavy yards of the past century.

Landscape architect Christy Ten Eyck allowed only one discrete piece of lawn to remain at her new Austin, Texas, home because it was a good spot for large family parties. She tidied up its formerly ratty edges by pulling in the sides and surrounding them with a crisply defined gravel walkway that creates a frame under the tall central oak.

One of the common denominators of a modern garden style is the absence of turf. Garden makers have known for decades that traditional lawns require large amounts of water, fertilizer, and pesticides to keep them looking pristine. These imported surfaces, vestiges of picturesque English pastures clipped by sheep, helped the colonists impose their idea of civilization on the wilderness. Somehow the perfect lawn, like big barbeque grills and oversize cars, has come to symbolize American patriotism and order. Lawn care—with all its attendant man-made products—stands as a bastion of masculinity in the realm of gardening, and powerful riding gas mowers have come to look more and more like macho SUVs. I wish I could report that the ideal of the impeccably mown lawn typified by the postwar suburban boom has gone the way of the Hummer, but as I travel around, I see that most American gardeners still fall back on a big expanse of bluegrass, or in Southern California they roll out Marathon, an unnaturally vivid sod.

With water restrictions and the growing concern for conservation of resources, some writers and designers are asking if any amount of lawn should be allowed these days, but I believe clipped grass has its place. As everyone remembers from childhood, grass is an excellent surface to play on. The notion of forcing kids to run around all day on gravel or concrete will never win out over our collective memories of bare feet in the cool grass on a hot day. And don't forget the appealing smell of freshly cut grass on a summer morning. If you have children around, a grassy area doesn't have to be as large as you might think. Nor does it need to be the blank canvas on which all of your property's features are arranged. Forward-thinking garden designers have come to include the lawn as just one of many optional elements in a landscape plan, like a wall, a terrace, a flowerbed, or a water feature. It's like thinking of turf as a rug—or even a sequence of rugs—instead of wall-to-wall carpeting.

Undeniably, the way we think about lawns has been shifting over the past several decades. For some, traditional turf has become a political lightning rod on the order of global warming and animal rights. Some zealous antilawn activists are determined to rid the world of its last clipped blade. Others would reasonably like to use less water and cut down on the weekly mow-and-blow maintenance bill. Regardless of where you fall on this spectrum, responsible homeowners should stop and consider their grass usage and question how much lawn, if any, is needed to fit the way they live or would like to live.

Driving around most city and suburban neighborhoods, you may notice a certain stylistic sameness. People are tribal, and most yards reveal that we like to belong. One idea or hybrid plant implemented during the postwar building spike in the 1950s may still be repeated endlessly today over many square blocks of a development like a persistent rumor. But things are changing as homeowners examine what our front yards, so long unconsidered and seemingly designed by rote, really say about ourselves both sociologically and environmentally.

The examples in this section address the notion of what it means to put a welcoming face on your home while keeping a firm hand on the environmental effects of your gardening activities. How much maintenance and machinery is involved? Does your yard waste water? Is it a haven for birds and other wildlife? These are the questions that the owner of the alternative lawn must address.

In Napa, California, Emmanuel Donval retained an elevated patch of lawn with gabion walls.

The Shrinking Lawn

Austin, Texas, isn't particularly known for its European-inspired gardens. That's not to say that there aren't plenty of stiffly clipped foundation shrubs and ho-hum symmetrical flowerbeds throughout the city's neighborhoods. But a gravel front yard filled with unusually trimmed topiary and a 32-foot-long ornamental pear allée and a well-loved but ever-shrinking amount of lawn in the back are rare enough in these quarters to draw attention.

Deborah Hornickel, a commercial real estate developer, bought her small postwar house in 1981 but didn't get around to tackling her overgrown 60- by 180-foot yard until a decade later. Confronted with a former rental property covered in weedy chinaberry and hackberry trees, the overwhelmed homeowner knew she needed help to define a garden out of this leafy mess. "I didn't have the funds to do much of anything, but I met James on a job and by chance he had just opened his store two blocks away. I told him I needed his help," Hornickel says. Luckily for Hornickel, the James in question was James David, an Austin landscape architect and former owner of the influential home-and-garden store Gardens. Over the past several decades, David has almost single-handedly transformed the way Austinites garden. "From the beginning, we did her garden the way I think is best: As money becomes available, we do another project," David says. "I don't like to think ahead of the money. A gardener has to be realistic."

He cleared the messy yard and installed two rows of saplings that would eventually form a tunnel-like allée of Bradford pears—a variety known for its dense upright growth but also for its habit of shedding branches during storms. (Branch loss hasn't

At Deborah Hornickel's Austin, Texas, stylishly formal backyard, she has preserved one last holdout of lawn, which is segregated from the rest of the garden by an allée of ornamental pear trees.

proved to be an issue here, perhaps because of rebar supports David added to the trees.) The designer can't recall the genesis of the idea for this formal design feature. "Maybe I saw we had extra pear trees in the nursery or something. I'm not sure why I thought of it," he says. "But I wanted to give the house some presence, and I have to say Deborah has always been up for most anything and so willing to experiment right from the start."

Ten 7-foot-tall, 1-inch caliper saplings that would form the allée looked fairly puny initially, especially spaced out every 8 feet, as David instructed. "It was a big stretch to imagine it ever looking good," Hornickel remembers. "I didn't understand what he was up to. But James was adamant, and we placed the saplings precisely by stringing a line and spacing them out at regular intervals." Within two seasons, as the trees grew and were trained over their arched supports, she realized how powerful their presence in her backyard would be and

how important it was to plan and measure everything out. "You can't be random with these sorts of formal features," she says. David showed her how to string a line down the long boxwood hedge so that the plants could be neatly clipped to the same level. But all this precision doesn't mean the yard is overly demanding in the amount of work that it requires. "People think that this garden must be incredibly high maintenance since it has clipped hedges and an allée, but really, once they're established, they don't require much work," she says, explaining further that she only trims the boxwood in spring and fall.

Above: Now that the pear trees have grown too large to form the perfectly symmetrical arch they once did, Deborah Hornickel cuts back any limbs that grow too low or in the wrong direction and allows the top to be wild and branchy. *Opposite:* A simple dining table and chair and a lily pool sit near to the allée and a patio of collaged salvage brick and stonework.

Hornickel and David possess strong opinions about the garden, and their discussions—though always friendly—sometimes get respectfully contentious when they don't see eye to eye on a project. "We argue a lot about what to do," David says. "Like when she cut down the huge magnolia in her front yard. But ultimately, she was right. It was out of scale with the house." David also keeps a wary eye on Hornickel's nursery visits. "She is a compulsive plant buyer," he says. "Especially in the front yard, where it sometimes teeters on the edge of looking like a big mess. But then she will pull it back." Hornickel validates that observation. "I do get too carried away sometimes," she admits with a good-natured shrug. But she has been editing, pulling out most of her early acquisitions—like the hybrid tea roses that required too much care and looked increasingly out of place.

Since it doesn't have a trace of lawn, Deborah Hornickel's front yard stands out on its residential block in downtown Austin. Boxwood cones and balls mix with other bits of eccentric plantings alongside a stone pathway: Here, a cloud of bronze fennel pops up—either by accident or design—between two topiaries; there, loose shrubs of smoke bush, vitex, and grevillea contrast with pots of squat agaves on stone plinths.

The pair has been friends for decades, and much of that time has been spent working on the garden. "Most Americans don't live in their houses very long, but we have been lucky enough to be able to develop our properties over many years," David says, alluding to his own Austin garden, perfected and expanded over the past 35 years. One of the ways both gardeners have altered their style is by selecting plants that do well in the hot, dry summers of Austin; another change has been to reduce or eliminate grass. In place of two large rectangles of lawn in the backyard, Hornickel remodeled a few years ago and expanded the gravel on one side. "James's idea," she reports. Gravel is indeed one of David's favorite materials, since he likes its feel underfoot and the blank canvas it gives for planting. "Texans only used to think of gravel as being for a cactus garden," he explains. "But I like to show how elegant it can be in different types of places."

Hornickel is justly proud of her garden and shares it with visitors on the Garden Conservancy's Open Days. Occasionally, she overhears comments from those who don't understand exactly where she's coming from. "Everyone gets so hung up on natives and xeriscaping and being absolutely correct," she says. "At first, they are surprised that the garden is so green and that I don't have a lot of bright salvias and ornamental grasses. On the other hand, sometimes they can't believe I have gravel and wonder where my St. Augustine lawn is." But she doesn't mind. Hornickel feels her garden is now fairly resolved, having successfully weathered a recent summer with a long run of 100-plus-degree temperatures and severe drought. Such a challenging weather pattern proves that this particular kind of European-inspired but forward-thinking garden can be fully at home in Central Texas.

Artificial Turf

The best examples of garden paving allow water to percolate down into the earth instead of directing it straight into the municipal gutter—or into the basement of a nearby house. However, some people still have a strong desire for the cool look and feel of a lawn. Many designers are experimenting with alternative ways of quite literally carpeting the garden. For instance, since grass never grew well in the small pocket garden behind their client's New York City townhouse because the surrounding buildings block the sunlight for most of the day, Susan Welti and Paige Keck of Foras Studio installed an artificial turf as a replacement. Welti says that every year new technologies make synthetic grass a more convincing substitute. The fake grass saves the money and maintenance of watering, the energy and pollution of mowing, and the often fruitless struggle of trying to grow sun-loving turf at the bottom of a dark city backyard. However, its use is best suited to a smaller, high-traffic, high-play area of the yard where a standard pristine lawn is desired.

Fake grass can make a viable substitute for real lawn in small areas that get little sunlight such as this one behind a New York City townhouse.

Where to Find It

EasyTurf
(www.easyturf.com)

ForeverLawn
(www.foreverlawn.com)

JM Synthetic Grass
(www.jmsyntheticgrass.com)

SynLawn
(www.synlawn.com)

Front Lawn Alternatives

In older neighborhoods where teardowns were the rule rather than the exception during the recent building boom, a relatively blank slate can be a welcome side effect of the sometimes wasteful destruction of an old house. This is an opportunity to carefully consider what goes into a site's design and what elements can make it more sustainable. Austin garden designer Mark Word is known for his sustainable approach, but he has faced resistance from some of his clients for using native species or other low-water plants in front gardens. They tend to worry that their property will look too scrappy and unkempt for the neighbors. Word takes a practical approach and uses his native plantings judiciously, as in this lawnless South Austin yard where he offsets their wilder appearance with strong design elements like a crisp-edged

walk of Texas limestone and planters of weathered steel backed by the imposing facade of a new house by Camille Jobe of Urban Jobe Architecture. Subtle leafy plants grown for their texture, such as sedges and yuccas, are accentuated by clumps of flowering oakleaf hydrangea, daylilies, and fox-tail lilies. The overall effect makes this front yard a new-style flower border instead of merely a patch of turf.

Instead of keeping the lawn relatively pristine and sacrosanct, as has been the norm, some gardeners are in favor of taking plantings right into the turf. In front of a house in Aspen, the homeowners added tulips, columbines, hardy geraniums, and even bold-leaved perennial ligularias to a romantically shaggy lawn of native buffalograss

In Austin, Texas, designer Mark Word made a front-yard garden of perennials and shrubs rather than the customary lawn.

Drought-Tolerant Grasses

Indian ricegrass (*Achnatherum hymenoides*)

Side oats grama (*Bouteloua curtipendula*)

Buffalograss (*Bouteloua dactyloides*)

Blue grama (*Bouteloua gracilis*)

Great basin wild rye (*Elymus cinereus*)

Arizona fescue (*Festuca arizonica*)

Blue fescue (*Festuca glauca*)

Idaho blue fescue (*Festuca idahoensis*)

Blue hair grass (*Koeleria glauca*)

Blue meadow grass (*Poa glauca* 'Blue Hills')

Little bluestem (*Schizachyrium scoparium*)

Blue-green moor grass (*Sesleria heufleriana*)

Prairie dropseed (*Sporobolus heterolepis*)

Available from Bluestem Nursery (www.bluestem.ca).

Note: Some grasses behave differently according to where they are grown; check with www.invasive.org to see which plants can cause trouble in your area.

A front yard in Aspen, Colorado, *opposite*, becomes a meadow of native buffalograss and flowering perennials. *Above:* Emmanuel Donval planted a small fenced yard in Napa with tall native tufted hairgrass.

(*Bouteloua dactyloides*). They also positioned a few granite boulders in among the scattered plants to create a stylized mountain meadow that, though far from authentic, seems entirely appropriate for the alpine town.

For a client in Napa, California, designer Emmanuel Donval removed a lawn and replaced it with simple rows of native or climate-suitable species of grasses. The fenced front yard of the 1852 house is so small it is was hardly worth the trouble to mow it. So Donval planted native tufted hairgrass (*Deschampsia caespitosa*) in strict rows that bring to mind the graphic arrangement of crops and vines in the countryside that surround the small, once agricultural town. The bunching clumps of perennial grass are cut back once a year so that the progression from spring green leaves to golden seed heads in late and summer and fall can be fully appreciated. This cutting is staggered in two groups (every other row) so that the first clumps have a head start to rebound and grow green leaves before the second group is cut.

CHAPTER 8

Recycling and Repurposing

ANOTHER METHOD OF making a garden that is less wasteful is to find ways to use, and even value, materials that many people normally discard without a second thought. Many gardeners are motivated by thrift and also by creativity and individualism and a desire to have garden spaces that look like no other place. It's the horticultural equivalent of a hip clothes shopper eschewing the mall for the secondhand shop.

The Art of Recycling

Shirley Watts, a San Francisco Bay Area garden designer, feels that she has gained the reputation as something of a green crusader by default because of her preference for recycling (or, in fact, reusing) found objects in her gardens. "I was brought up that way in Philadelphia," she says. "My parents were children of the Great Depression, so we were always going to thrift stores and finding things as part of a natural conservatism. I was taught something is much more special if you find it instead of just going to the store and buying it new." But it's not just Watts who is looking for ways to create gardens out of materials that don't come bought from run-of-the-mill home centers.

Bay Area designer Shirley Watts made a screen of discarded computer motherboards, *opposite*, for a garden in Berkeley, California, that also included recycled glass mulch, *above*.

Shirley Watts, who has been gardening in Alameda with her mathematician husband, Emmanuel Coup, since the early 1990s, is known around San Francisco and its highly creative environs for the unconventional and sometimes provocative materials she uses in her garden. Her aesthetic fits within the inventive, often wacky funk art movement that came out of the 1960s and '70s, especially in the Bay Area. The spirit of that movement and its almost surrealistic appreciation for found objects can be found in a

Over time, the reclaimed motherboards in this garden screen have formed a patina in shades of copper, green, and blue.

loose cadre of area gardeners known as the Hortisexuals, a group of which Watts is a member. Her design work fits somewhat into the same vein as eccentric Bay Area garden makers like Marcia Donohue and Bob Clark, who are known for incorporating ribald ceramic art, industrial salvage, and unexpected garden ornaments like bowling balls, teacups, marbles, and wine bottles into their gardens. Watts's work seems to have more of a modernist's rigor, but she disagrees with that observation. "People think of my gardens as being contemporary," she says, "but I don't think of myself as a modernist. For me, finding something to reuse in a creative way gives a space some sense of history."

Watts, who enjoys the creativity of designing installations for garden shows, teamed up with a cabinetmaker named Ross Craig to do an exhibit at the San Francisco Garden Show in 2003. Afterward, parts of that garden were dismantled and reinstalled in Craig's tiny Berkeley backyard. The main feature here is a metal screen: One graphic panel consists of several dozen reclaimed computer motherboards, and the other is a recirculating water feature that trickles sensuously down a stainless steel screen from a dribbling pipe. Though she was questioned several times at the garden show about the idea of reusing motherboards, which contain heavy metals, Watts had already thought it through. "We're not growing tomatoes or anything edible under them," she explains. "So I don't think it would be any better to send them to China so that they could be burnt. I think they are fine being used here, since absolutely nobody wants to deal with them."

Oddly enough, this bit of high-tech refuse from the information age blends seamlessly in the shady, moist garden, partially obscured by the surrounding dwarf tree ferns (*Blechnum gibbum* 'Silver Lady') and a large clumping timber bamboo (*Bambusa oldhamii*), whose thick green culms are dusted with their own pale blue patina. The garden's patio is made of

Above: Garden designer Shirley Watts at her Alameda, California, studio. Opposite: For Karen Evind, Watts made fences of collaged vinyl billboards that she rescued as they were headed to the landfill.

different-size squares of pigmented concrete interspersed with gaps of tumbled glass recycled from old streetlights. The small garden is as much for sitting in as it is for viewing from the large picture window inside the small house.

A long fence that runs down one side of the yard is yet another distinctive aspect of the garden. Watts, who is always looking for new ways to screen out the neighbors of her clients' gardens, wanted to make the nondescript wooden enclosure more interesting. So she wrapped it with large strips of discarded vinyl billboards. The resulting pop art mural is reminiscent of the large, colorfully fragmented canvases of artist James Rosenquist. "When I was an artist, I used to do a lot of collage work, and I thought it would be cool to use actual billboards," Watts says. After a series of failed attempts to connect with a good source for the

discarded signage, Watts found an employee of a display advertising business who finally returned her call and allowed her to come down to the sign company to pick up what they considered to be garbage. The folded pieces can weigh around 150 pounds, and when unfolded they might be 24 by 72 feet. "That's bigger than my backyard," Watts notes, saying that she usually cuts up these large pieces in the parking lot of her studio with a pair of scissors. Since most billboards are up only for 6 to 8 weeks, there is a lot of discarded imagery to choose from, including the movie posters that provide her favorite pictorial themes.

For a simple backyard redesign for Karen Evind in San Rafael, Watts went with a subtler, less pop-oriented approach by choosing imagery in muted shades. "When it's

Left: A collection of salvaged metal, tires, and lettering from commercial signage transforms Emmanuel Donval's driveway into a gravel cactus garden of surreal elements. *Overleaf:* Donval made a vertical pocket garden out of metal roof jacks and planted the vents with a mixture of colorful succulents.

some movie actor I wasn't familiar with," Watts remembers. "Karen recognized him immediately and wasn't so happy that he would be staring at her all the time. She was totally right, so it came down." A few bits of *Catwoman* imagery also had to be removed, since they looked a little too S/M even after they had been sliced and diced.

For Watts, making a garden isn't all about "reuse, renew, and recycle." "I seem to have this reputation as the Queen of Recycling," she says, "but that's not really what I'm about. It's a gut thing for me. I like to play with geometry and curves just as if I were sculpting or painting." Watts's gardens have become her art form and a mode of self-expression. "It's more than setting out to do good in the world with recycling," she says. "I wasn't even that good a painter, to be honest. I'm better at making gardens—and I get so much more satisfaction doing it."

In the large driveway leading to a wooden garage, Emmanuel Donval has made a quirky gravel garden of recycled and reused materials at his Napa home. He constructed a wall from a mixture of salvaged and new roof jacks, which usually function as metal flashing for roof vents, and screwed them together to form a wall with plantable pockets where the designer could experiment with growing hardy succulents without irrigation. Salvaged signs from an Albertsons grocery store and planters made from screwed-together stacks of reused car, motorcycle, and scooter tires give the garden a surrealistic, and somehow quirkily Gallic, air.

successful, the photographs give a whole other depth to the garden," she says. "It doesn't stop your eye like a blank wall would; instead, it allows it to continue on." Evind gave Watts free rein to use whatever billboard imagery inspired her, but once she started stapling the pieces on the wooden frame, a couple of problems came up for the homeowner. "Karen was really great. Then I put up a section with a large face from

Opposite: Los Angeles designer Jay Griffith created a tall screen of found materials to frame a cattle-tank fishpond planted with water lilies and papyrus. The water circulates from the pond through an overflowing ceramic planter that sits in the water. *Above:* At the same garden, Griffith screened off a utility area from an outdoor daybed with painted pieces of salvaged wood and metal arranged in graphic stripes.

It takes an artist's eye to see advantage in the debris left behind on a construction site and transform it into something beautiful. When Jay Griffith helped Ian Kimbrey and Joanne Forchas-Kimbrey pull together their small Venice, California, garden backyard after a big renovation, he found a trove of useful scrap wood and corrugated metal. He painted the long wooden planks that had been used for concrete forms various shades of green and combined them with surplus galvanized metal roofing panels to create distinctively striped garden dividers. Like folding screens in a house, these collaged panels make a backdrop for a water tank lily pond and an outdoor patio but also conceal a work area for the couple, both avid organic gardeners. Obviously, Griffith—who is well-known for his flair with found and flea market objects—has the eye to pull this off. But given similar raw materials, even less-creative types can take a page from this inventive solution for their gardens by looking at what others might discard as possible media for artistic expression.

Edible Gardens and Community

PART III

CHAPTER 9

Growing Food at Home

THE PROBLEM FOR most city dwellers, children and adults alike, is that we are so far removed from our food sources. We're surrounded by farms, but they are usually many miles away, and while farmers' markets are indeed a wonderful way to find locally sourced food, we don't get to see how the produce is being grown there. It's important for people to witness how food is cultivated firsthand. Searching for a way to do this in an urban environment can lead to some fascinating situations.

Homeowners like Emmanuel Donval in Napa, California, *opposite*, are going to great lengths to be a part of the local food movement, from front-yard kitchen gardens to backyard chicken coops.

Backyard Economics

The concept of edible gardening brings up an interesting discussion. For most people, just how sustainable is growing vegetables at home? How much food can a modern gardener—who works elsewhere for her means—grow in a limited space? How much does that produce cost per pound when you factor in the time and labor it required? There is also the question of whether or not growing small amounts of food unduly consumes resources, manpower, and fertilizer compared to, for example, a low-water garden. Is it better simply to pool our resources and buy vegetables from local large-scale growers who have everything down to a science of productivity? Experts with more knowledge and experience than I, the most widely read being author Michael Pollan, have dealt with many of these questions and issues elsewhere. Meanwhile, clever Web sites like Homegrown Evolution (www.homegrownevolution.com) and Civil Eats (http://civileats.com) have documented what it's like to "grow your own" from a personal, decidedly urban standpoint. I will leave the complicated equations and economics to them. What I'd like to express is this simple

affirmation: Growing, harvesting, cooking, and eating something that you've grown—no matter how tiny the yield—is one of the most important, and nearly lost, of human art forms.

Take what Michelle Obama has done with the White House vegetable garden. Of course, no one is trying to convince the public that the produce from that small plot entirely sustains even one member of the first family or their many guests for even a week. Critics may say she is doing it for just for PR or that she is exercising some sort of rural, of-the-people fantasy à la Marie Antoinette at her fake farmhouse. But that's not the point. The inarguably glamorous first lady is a powerful role model when she digs around in the dirt with groups of schoolchildren and shows them where lettuces come from— not bound with rubber bands and encased in plastic bubbles at the supermarket, but right from the earth. In this modern-day victory garden, she reveals to them an ancient art, and she does so not as an expert but as an active participant who wants to eat better and consider where her food comes from.

My own journey to loving vegetables was long and troubled but distinctly influenced by local agriculture. I grew up with canned food and therefore harbored a deep-seated childhood hatred and mistrust of most vegetables, including all forms of asparagus, spinach, and peas. It's no accident that the only vegetables I liked were the fresh corn, onions, black-eyed peas, limas, and okra that my dad grew in our backyard or bought from farmers' roadside stands during the summer. That's a valuable lesson for every parent. When you are a child, there is something very scary about a beet if you've never seen one in its natural habitat.

A working vegetable garden can be as ornamental as a traditional flower garden. In Nantucket, Laura Simon and her family have been growing much of their food for several decades.

A Family "Farm"

"Our garden is a big part of our world," Jennifer Dibs says of her small property tucked into a hillside across from the Silver Lake Reservoir in Los Angeles. In that enviable way of Southern Californians, she and her family (her partner, Mary Ann Dibs, and their two teenage daughters, Barbara and Tina) spend as much time outdoors as indoors. They have transformed what could have been an ordinary urban yard into a kind of family animal farm with chickens, rabbits, and fish. Jennifer, a dog walker by profession, has loved animals since childhood. Unlike many homeowners, she doesn't begrudge even the wildest species that comes calling, whether it's a gopher digging up the flowerbeds, the skunk out front, or the various raccoons and opossums that climb around the backyard arbor when the grapevines are heavy with fragrant fruit. "I don't mind them at all," Jennifer says. "In fact, I love that they come by."

Several years ago, the couple bought chickens to give the girls the experience of raising poultry (these were added to the rabbits and guinea pigs they already had). The three Silkie hens, "the lapdogs of the chicken world," as Jennifer calls them, are sweet but not very good egg producers and spend their time following the family around or sitting on fallen lemons in the yard. "They are better brooders than layers," she sighs, adding that she'd like to get some Rhode Island Reds for the sake of productivity. After having several friends lose their chickens to wild animals in the most upsetting way, Jennifer and Mary Ann installed a "super-duper secure coop" with three or four latches to thwart the most dexterous raccoon and a solid bottom to defend the hens from the animals that come digging around at night. So far, there have been no casualties.

The family accomplished quite a lot in the narrow outdoor spaces surrounding their old world–looking stucco cottage, which, along with several others in their neighborhood, was built by a Swiss émigré architect in 1926. When the couple moved in 15 years ago, they found the usual overgrown backyard and a sloped front yard that was a boring monoculture of ivy. They terraced the front with railroad ties to create flat beds that now contain a wild combination of tough native and imported plants. Huge fuzzy-leaved stands of mauve Canary Island sage (*Salvia canariensis*) that can grow to 8 feet in a season compete with orange lion's ear (*Leonotis leonurus*) and the California native matilija poppy (*Romneya coulteri*). Nearby, *Iochroma cyanea,* a leggy shrub from South America, is covered with deep purple trumpets that are a favorite of hummingbirds. Jennifer is loath to prune back this vivid thicket too hard or with much frequency, since it sustains so many animals and birds. But before the winter rains, she and Mary Ann cut back enough to keep it looking manageable (and enough to fill their compost bins to the brim). The whole planting is designed to be drought tolerant if not drought proof. In fact, there was a 2- or 3-year period where the seldom-used sprinkler system was not functioning, and only a couple of plants were lost. "It's pretty Darwinian out there," she admits, though at the time, the garden didn't look so great.

In the back, Jennifer and Mary Ann limbed up the existing gnarled trees and lanky abutilons and built a simple wooden arbor that they planted with a 'Thompson Seedless' grape. This shades an outdoor dining area furnished with several comfortable couches for reading. "Having the girls changed our outlook on what we wanted to the backyard to

In the Silver Lake neighborhood of Los Angeles, Jennifer and Mary Ann Dibs and their daughters, *opposite*, tend vegetables, fruit, chickens for the eggs, and rabbits (the latter not to eat) in a small backyard.

look like," says Jennifer. "Originally, we wanted a Zen kind of gravel garden, but we realized that they needed a place to play, so we added a fake lawn." She says that even though more and more of her neighbors are getting into dry gardening, some of them are still puzzled by the artificial lawn. "They think it's inconceivable that I call myself a gardener and then have something fake in the yard," she says. "But grass in Los Angeles just doesn't make sense to me."

In the past several years, the side yard has been turned into a kitchen garden full of herbs, berries, and vegetables for the two girls, who enjoy gardening "more than teenagers are supposed to," Jennifer says. Mary Ann loves to clear overgrown plants and tends to the compost pile. Jennifer makes a point to sit out in the garden doing nothing for 10 or 15 minutes every day. "Instead of meditating or yoga," she explains. "I just try to be as quiet as possible without bringing anything with me to read or to work on. I just don't do anything but look at the garden and observe." For her, it's important that whatever the family does on the site will not harm the space. "I consider this place to be borrowed and that I'm going to return it one day in good shape," she says. "In the meantime, I want to make it be pretty while we're here."

The Dibs family's small backyard hosts a lot of outdoor living, from viola practice, *above left*, to open-air dinners under the grape arbor, *opposite top*, to picking fresh greens from the herb garden, *opposite bottom left*. Jennifer Dibs, *opposite bottom right*, admires the front-yard jungle of purple salvias and orange lion's ear, with its views of the reservoir. Tall white matilija poppy grows along the sidewalk.

Enriching the Soil

A more traditional vegetable garden in Nantucket is one of the most inspiring that I've ever had the chance to visit. Not only is it impressive because of the seemingly flawless condition of its plants—on my visit there was not a yellowed or bug-eaten leaf in sight—but also because its owner, Laura Simon, says she doesn't follow any set rules other than being completely organic.

Simon has lived at her rural house with its fenced, ⅓-acre garden since 1983. That's a good amount of time to perfect one's gardening skills. But as Thomas Jefferson, her imaginary correspondent in her 1999 book *Dear Mr. Jefferson: Letters from a Nantucket Gardener,* wrote in a letter of 1811:

No occupation is so delightful to me as the culture of the earth, and no culture comparable to that of the garden. Such a variety of subjects, some one always coming to perfection, the failure of one thing repaired by the success of another, and instead of one harvest a continued one through the year. Under a total want of demand except for our family table, I am still devoted to the garden. But though an old man, I am but a young gardener.

The author still has a long way to go before she approaches Jefferson's nearly 70 years of age when he wrote that letter to his friend, the artist and naturalist Charles Willson Peale. Every gardener, no matter his or her time in life, can identify with that last sentence. There is just too much to learn and know about tending plants to cram in one lifetime. Simon's letters to Jefferson recount not only the decades she has spent in her garden but also the challenges of growing vegetables on an island in the Atlantic. Simon is as passionate

Starting Seeds Indoors

Everything, except for the strawberries and potatoes, is grown from seeds started indoors by Laura Simon and her husband, Tom—several thousand seedlings in all. She recommends two favorite seed companies. Fedco Seeds (www.fedcoseeds.com), from Maine, sells non–genetically modified varieties, and she also enjoys Fragrant Path (www.fragrantpathseeds.com), another catalog that sells unusual seed varieties, especially annual flowers. March through June, the bed in her guest bedroom is moved against the wall and grow lights are suspended over a worktable full of dozens of flats of seedlings that will be moved out into a garden shed or cold frames. The young plants finally go out into the garden after the last frost.

Laura Simon's Nantucket garden, above, is sustained by strict organic practices and generous applications of horse manure.

about her garden as Jefferson seems to have been about his, and she shares his inclination for precise record keeping. After she and I discussed the garden at length on the telephone, she sent me the following e-mail to further outline what was going on in her garden during winter:

Stephen, as often happens when asked "What's in the garden?" my mind went temporarily blank. While it's true, as I told you, that there are leeks, carrots (3 varieties), kale (4 varieties), and lettuce (4 varieties) still in the ground, we are also eating vegetables stored in the cellar and the freezer. We have potatoes (11 varieties), sweet potatoes (3 varieties and a 5-variety sampler of heirlooms), winter squash (3 varieties), as well as acorn squash (2) onions (yellow and red, but the shallots didn't make it to maturity this year), and garlic (3 varieties). In the frozen department are blueberries (the strawberries—2 varieties—succumbed to mold and the raspberries—yellow and red—were polished off with the Christmas crepes), sweet and hot peppers (not sure how many varieties, but lots), and Swiss chard, but no tomatoes, though I salvaged just enough to make 15 batches of ratatouille. I can't tell you what a treat it is to taste the flavors of summer on a bleak winter night. And let's not forget the popcorn.

"The first tenet is to build the soil," Simon says, crediting the robust health of her plants to the richness of the simple planting beds that she has carved out of turf. "It was okay when we first got it, but after 20 years of amending, it's really beautiful." Like Jefferson, she spends a lot of time thinking about compost, crop rotations, and soil amendments. Every spring, the garden gets top-dressed with 3 inches of composted horse manure that she gathers from several nearby stables, where she has a standing order to take all that they can produce. "Every year, one thing or another doesn't do so well, but that's all to do with the weather," Simon says. "One year, it was cold and rainy all of June, so we

didn't eat a single strawberry. And what things we did get lacked flavor since the sun wasn't there to bake the flavor into them."

Tending a large amount of gardening space is undeniably a lot of work. Simon and her husband do most of it but call in help for some of the weeding. Needless to say, Simon reports that she never has to buy vegetables at the grocery store, and any surplus goes to friends and family. She and her husband eat seasonally all year long. "When the asparagus is in, we eat it every night for 6 or so weeks," she says. "Then we don't eat it at all till it comes back around again." Even during the winter cold, Simon and her husband continue to enjoy their harvest. A 6-inch layer of straw protects the beds, and certain vegetables continue to thrive under Agribon AG-19 floating row covers from Johnny's Selected Seeds or under an insulating blanket of snow. Once more, Simon credits the all-important base of healthy soil that helps make her agricultural pursuits easier. She quotes from a letter that Jefferson wrote to his daughter Martha in 1793: "We will try this winter to cover our garden with a heavy coating of manure. When the earth is rich it bids defiance to droughts, yields in abundance, and of the best quality." As Simon notes, that's the whole story right there.

Chickens peck away near neat rectangular beds of white-flowered potatoes, *above*, and asparagus, *opposite*, at Laura Simon's garden.

The Urban Theorists

Callie Janoff's and Randall Stoltzfus's small backyard in Crown Heights, Brooklyn, is not the sort of sleekly designed space you might see behind other newly renovated brownstones in their rapidly changing borough. "For us, it's more about the experience of gardening than it is about what it looks like at any given moment," Stoltzfus says. There was no professional garden designer at work here; Janoff and Stoltzfus did it all themselves with an almost obsessive intellectual curiosity and rigor. When Janoff bought and moved into the fairly derelict commercial property that once housed an office, the couple found a backyard that had suffered from years of neglect. That first season, they decided just to watch the yard to see what plants came up, only to realize they had a garden of weeds. "Our first visitors had to pick the cockleburs off their clothes after being out in the yard," Janoff remembers. After clearing the small but valuable space, they started by discussing what the parameters for their garden would be. Perhaps because both grew up around edible gardens, the couple agreed that their backyard needed to produce food. Janoff spent summers with her father in Chicago, where she picked lettuces and greens every night before dinner. Stoltzfus, who comes from a Mennonite farming background, grew up with a home vegetable garden in rural Virginia.

To avoid any possible toxins lurking in the old soil of their urban backyard, the couple made raised beds, repurposing all the bits of concrete and masonry that they excavated to avoid hauling them away. To these beds, they added new soil and lots of compost from a now-defunct giveback program that allowed New York City gardeners the chance to pick up free compost made from chipped Christmas trees and leaves.

The couple soon began exploring the concepts of permaculture, an ecological movement begun in the 1970s and defined by its creator, Bill Mollison, as "a design system

Randall Stoltzfus, an artist, and Callie Janoff, a seminary student, *opposite top,* have turned their tiny, shaded Brooklyn backyard into a personal laboratory to try out some rather advanced horticulture concepts such as small-scale permaculture and food growing. Their garden provides them with joy that is not only aesthetic or culinary, like strawberries, *opposite,* and mint, *below,* but also intellectual.

for creating sustainable human environments." That concept is simple enough, but as you delve deeper and read more about permaculture, the idea becomes more multilayered and difficult to define to a novice. I admit that sometimes I struggle with the meaning of the word. It's simplest to think of permaculture as a concept that allows us to design landscapes modeled on the self-sustaining interrelationships between aspects of nature—including animals and humans. It is a theory of linked systems. To educate themselves, Stoltzfus and Janoff started with Mollison's two classic texts, *Permaculture One* and *Permaculture Two*. Finding those books a little daunting, the couple discovered a couple of more manageable titles that were helpful in trying to decide how to apply these broad, often rangy concepts in their small space.

Meanwhile, Janoff dotes on her favorite plants: a white raspberry that she bought at the Brooklyn Botanic Garden plant sale and the various herbs (such as lemon verbena and holy basil) she uses almost daily for tea. Stoltzfus loves the kiwi vine and the almost too-vigorous Jerusalem artichokes—he dug up one 4-pound clump of tubers last summer. A volunteer butternut squash, which snaked across the small central patio as if it were heading into the house, yielded four full-size squash. Herbs are some of their most useful plants: fennel for its seed, lots of mint, sorrel, mustard, stevia for sweetening, and scented geraniums.

Stoltzfus, an artist, and Janoff, a seminary student, do their garden on a tight budget, with little financial outlay for equipment or products. "With food gardens, it's not about consumption in a consumer sense, it's about production," Janoff says. They know they will never be able to feed themselves exclusively from their tiny plot, but the positive effects of being consistently drawn outside during the growing season to tend the garden remain undeniable.

An Urban Food Grower's Reading List

- **Perennial Vegetables: From Artichokes to Zuiki Taro, a Gardener's Guide to over 100 Delicious and Easy to Grow Edibles,** by Eric Toensmeier, explains the permaculture of planting edible plants that don't have to be sown every year. It inspired Brooklyn gardeners Callie Janoff and Randall Stoltzfus to create a small backyard water garden, where they grow watercress.

- **Fresh Food from Small Places: The Square Inch Gardener's Guide to Year-Round Growing, Fermenting, and Sprouting,** by R. J. Ruppenthal, is a book that Stoltzfus says is "aimed squarely at urban gardeners."

- **Gaia's Garden: A Guide to Home-Scale Permaculture,** by Toby Hemenway, discusses elements of permaculture in a residential setting.

In the Janoff/Stoltzfus garden, even the small water feature, *opposite*, supplies food: edible watercress. In raised beds, a variety of unusual herbs are grown for salads and tea.

At the home of a client in Austin, Texas, landscape designer Robert Leeper turned a barren side yard into an elegant kitchen garden, opposite, using raised beds of rough-hewn blocks of local Hill Country limestone. The white stone, long a part of the building vernacular of many neighborhoods around Austin, is inexpensive and easy to work with. Leeper likes its formal qualities, which become visually invaluable when the garden is a bit overgrown at the end of the season or when the beds are fallow. He feels that the thick stone keeps the beds moister and cooler in the heat of the summer. Durability is an added plus; unlike wood, the limestone will not rot or need to be replaced so quickly.

Raised Beds

Installing beds that sit above ground level, like those at the Janoff/Stoltzfus garden, is a lot like gardening in containers. Both methods give a greater level of control over the quality of the soil, and that's important in urban sites where you're not sure what terrible things might have happened on your property in the past. For instance, a backyard could have once sat next door to an industrial operation or been the dumping ground for a century's worth of lead-based paint. There are many schools of thought about raised beds. For decades, John Jeavons, a Northern California gardener and author of *How to Grow More Vegetables: And Fruits, Nuts, Berries, Grains, and Other Crops Than You Ever Thought Possible on Less Land Than You Can Imagine,* has been promoting a systematic approach to raised beds derived from the theories of two past gurus of organic gardening, Alan Chadwick of University of

California, Santa Cruz and the mystical Austrian philosopher and biodynamic agriculturalist Rudolf Steiner. Some might find Jeavons's principles of sustainable "biointensive mini-farming" to be overkill for a small backyard. He insists on double-digging—a practice where the soil is excavated down two spade heights (about 2 feet) before being amended with organic soil conditioners and replaced and mounded in unedged beds.

Another approach comes via Mel Bartholomew, who expounds his own system of "square-foot gardening" in his books and on a Web site. He gave up on backbreaking double-digging years ago and now favors constructing an open-bottomed box of lumber fitted with a 1- by 1-foot grid that is placed on top of the lawn or existing soil. For most gardeners, perhaps the most advantageous path lies somewhere between the two

experts. Both methods basically involve a lot of upfront labor that is later rewarded by the superior harvest and minimal weeding that comes once the beds are established.

- Begin by taking string and wooden stakes and laying out the size and number of beds you'll need—one to two squares or rectangles are usually a good start.

- Don't make your beds any wider than 4 feet, since you'll want to easily reach the interior of the beds without having to step inside. The whole idea of a raised bed is to keep the soil light, loose, and untrampled while you weed and plant. Also make sure the path between the beds is wide enough to easily access all sides.

- Build the sides of your beds to 6 to 8 inches in height out of stones, bricks, or rot-resistant lumber like cedar secured with stakes and rust-proof hardware. Avoid using pressure-treated wood that can contain

harmful preservatives, even arsenic. Less-expensive types of lumber, like pine, ultimately degrade but can last for a decade.

- If you want to keep your new vegetables' roots from reaching into the original, less-desirable soil, make deeper planters and lay down a semipermeable weed barrier (www.planetnatural.com/site/weed-barrier.html) that allows water and air to pass through.

And if you still have reason to be worried about the toxicity of your soil, then it's best to get professional advice. Contact your local Cooperative Extension agent (www.csrees.usda.gov/Extension) to see about getting your soil tested. If it's contaminated above acceptable levels, you may decide to have the top layer removed. But hopefully, just raising the level of your planting area will get the situation under control.

CHAPTER 10

Raising Chickens and Livestock in the City

IF SOMEONE HAD taken me aside at a party back in 2005 and whispered, "Chicken coops . . . chicken coops are going to be a big trend," I would have been incredulous, to say the least. During that first decade of the millennium, as everyone was trying to flash as much money and expensive possessions as possible, it would have been nearly inconceivable to imagine urban hipsters becoming earnest backyard poultry enthusiasts. But it has happened.

Chickens Come to Roost

You know a trend has fully unfurled when the *New York Times* publishes a trend backlash story, as they did in an October 2009 article about the people who were regretting their backyard chickens. Those interviewed said the birds were too much trouble and that they found the various chicken diseases disgusting. The article quoted a representative of an animal rescue group who said they were having to deal with a large number of abandoned chickens, especially noisy roosters who were thought to be hens when they were purchased as chicks.

Chickens provide eggs and lots of personality to Marion Brenner's Berkeley backyard, *opposite*. In Portland, Emily Gowen shares a family of goats in a cooperative setup with her neighbors, *right*.

As with most trends, there is a sort of hipster bell curve. The baseline of the curve is formed of a smallish group of people who are doing a particular nonfashionable something, and most likely they've been doing it for years. Perhaps they are knitting or ironically sporting a moustache, or both. When influential early adopters "discover" the activity and promote it as new and desirable, more and more people take it up. Fairly soon the population gets saturated, and eventually disillusionment sets in for the trendiest part of the group. Either the style loses its luster, or the activity proves to be more difficult or less satisfying than many people expected. Ultimately, participation decreases, and the wave subsides nearly to the point at which it started, leaving a group of dedicated folks who just might end up staying with the practice. After spending some time with the following group of backyard poultry and livestock lovers, I tend to think they will stick with their furred and feathered charges for the long term.

The Ornamented Farm

On a downtown lot in Napa, California, garden designer Emmanuel Donval and his partner, Dan Worden, have taken their ordinary front and back yards and turned them into multifunctional food-producing spaces in the 18th-century French and English tradition of the *ferme ornée* (or ornamental farm), where beauty and utility hold nearly equal importance. These ideas start right in front of the 1932 house, where Donval removed the lawn in the small yard and made a garden that emphasized edibles. A white picket fence fits into the traditional style of the neighborhood, but inside its confines, things get adventurous. Donval lined the fence with blueberries, raspberries, and currants in narrow beds edged with gravel paths. He removed the straight concrete front walk, stacking up the pieces like blocks so that they could be reused as a garden bench. The seat is backed by pear trees that are espaliered (trained to grow

flat) on a metal-and-wire frame. Bending the branches in this way encourages fruiting buds to form all along the horizontal branches, so the technique is not merely decorative but efficient in a smaller garden. Other frost-hardy fruit trees include persimmons and the jelly date palm (*Butia capitata*), a heavy fruiting tree from the dry grasslands of South America that is popular in California and across the southern United States.

Donval, a native of Bordeaux and Évian-les-Bains, France, started his design business named Green Cherry in 2006 after working for several well-known Bay Area designers. He now focuses on designing smaller residential projects where he can actively be on-site and involved with the gardens that he creates while exploring his ideas of food growing and sustainability. His main laboratory for these concepts is right in his own yard. The large year-round kitchen garden of beans, tomatoes, carrots, beets, eggplants, and melons is laid out in the somewhat formal style of a French potager, where the inclusion of flowers gives the vegetable garden a highly ornamental look. Its tall sunflowers and single-petaled dahlias attract pollinators from his nearby beehives. Every year, Donval says, he tries a new vegetable. One year it was chickpeas, another it was salsify. He plans to try lentils next.

Chickens are one of Donval's favorite aspects of his urban homestead. He keeps three of them—Coco, Sophie, and Samantha—in a portable chicken tractor inspired by Michael Pollan's description of Joel Salatin's version in *The Omnivore's Dilemma*. Donval and Worden designed it by combining several different models that they admired on www.chickentractorplans.com. The resulting self-contained wooden and metal chicken coop may be moved around the lawn to give the birds fresh insect pecking ground while they fertilize the grass with their droppings. After a full day of eating grass and bugs, the chickens retire to the enclosed second-

Emmanuel Donval remade his ordinary front yard into a kitchen garden by removing the lawn and adding small fruit trees and berry bushes. To create more space, he removed the concrete sidewalk and stacked the pieces to make a bench.

Beekeeping Resources

Emmanuel Donval recommends these books for new apiarists:

- *The Beekeeper's Handbook*, by Alphonse Avitabile and Diana Sammataro
- *Beekeeping for Dummies*, by Howland Blackiston

He suggests that those interested in learning more about bees should join the bee-keeping association in their county. He feels local training is the best way to learn most quickly about what can be highly specific conditions and resources.

In the backyard, Emmanuel Donval grows vegetables, keeps honeybees, and raises chickens that travel around the lawn in a mobile chicken tractor coop.

floor coop at one end of the tractor. Donval moves the device approximately every other day so that the grass does not get overgrazed and scratched up by the chickens. The garden's large lawn has been a source of concern for Donval over the years, since it does require regular mowing and water. But he feels that it is a highly productive yard for his birds, who he thinks are "among the happiest chickens on earth," yielding 14 to 21 eggs a week for the couple and their friends. Donval feeds his chickens a mixture of corn and discarded salad greens salvaged from the bins of a nearby supermarket. They haven't had to deal with the issue of nonlaying chickens yet, but when it happens, Donval will take a Frenchman's pragmatic approach: He looks forward to making a *poule au pot* (boiled chicken) of any bird that is too old to be roasted.

At the rear of the garden, Donval keeps two beehives. One is a feral swarm that he relocated to his backyard as part of a local program. He is registered with the county to rescue troublesome swarms from homes whose owners want to get rid of unwanted bees. The second is a split from the first hive. Initially attracted to beekeeping when he wanted to learn more about pollinators, Donval learned the craft by taking classes from a beekeeping club in San Francisco. He stopped buying expensive commercial bees when he realized that the feral swarms needed homes. Some years, he collects as much as 30 pounds of well-flavored honey.

Donval is always experimenting with new gardening techniques, new mulches, and new materials to lessen his workload and increase his productivity. He says he spends 30 minutes to an hour in the garden every morning, with 2 or 3 hours allotted for more involved tasks every other week. This direct sense of involvement keeps him in tune with what he can reasonably expect from his clients in terms of maintenance on their own gardens. But it is this strong connection to a sense of place and the passage of time in his garden that keeps him interested in gardening and growing the food that he is proud to bring to the table.

For the Love of Chickens

Longtime Berkeley, California, resident Marion Brenner is a relatively new convert to the world of chickens, but for her, keeping poultry is more than a passing fancy. In 2006, she and her husband, Robert Shimshak, built a coop of recycled redwood, salvaged windows, and wire at the top of their sloped 1-acre lot. Brenner, a photographer, started raising chickens to provide manure for her vegetable garden more than she did for the eggs. Now she loves gathering the 20 to 30 eggs that her Araucanas, Rhode Island Reds, and Silver Laced Wyandottes lay every week. Far from being a farm girl herself (she grew up in suburban Westchester County just north of New York City), Brenner considers her chickens working animals rather than pets and has therefore never named them. Nor has she reconciled in her mind the questions concerning when (and how) a person gets rid of old, nonlaying birds. It's a quandary that separates many city people from their more pragmatic brethren on the farm. Most chickens start laying at around 6 months but after anywhere from 2 to 5 years, they begin to be less productive. Traditionally, of course, these nonlaying birds are eaten without a second thought. But for most of us, animal slaughter is no longer part of our day-to-day lives.

Unlike the constituents of the chicken backlash, Brenner doesn't find her birds to be an unsatisfying amount of trouble, though she admits in a smaller space they might do some damage to plantings. She had to fence off her vegetable patch, since the chickens go right for her lettuces and any green leaves (pea vines, broccoli, and cauliflower are big hits). She cleans out the nesting boxes every week, and once every few weeks she rakes out the pen and throws in some new mulch. As for the manure, the initial reason she started with the chickens, she ages it for 3 to 6 months in compost bins, and she reports that her vegetables love the extra nourishment from their rich soil. By Berkeley city ordinance, all food waste must be composted, so Brenner either

Berkeley, California, has strict rules on garbage disposal. Between her home composting regimen for her organic garden, *opposite top*, and her chickens, Marion Brenner carries just a tiny bag of trash out to the sidewalk bin each week.

composts hers in bins or feeds it to her chickens. They love her table scraps: corncobs (their favorite dish), rice, onions, salad greens, and most any tired vegetables from the refrigerator. Nothing goes to waste. Consequently, Brenner says she doesn't have much garbage anymore.

Brenner has found the birds to be pleasant additions to the rhythm of her day as she lets them out of their pen to peck around the yard. She finds their strict social order fascinating, and she's educating herself by reading books and talking to a neighbor, her "chicken guru." Even though she stops short of describing them as pets, Brenner admits that her chickens are wonderfully cheerful company as they accompany her while she works in the garden, gathering round to see what she digs up. The animals add a sense of life to her garden that was lacking before—one that now she can't imagine gardening without.

The Farm and Feed Store Gets Hip

Berkeley, California, and Portland, Oregon, share certain similarities. To the casual visitor, they both seem to have a large population of politically left-leaning, community-minded gardeners. They both appear to have a fondness for backyard chickens. Where there are chicken enthusiasts, there must be stores to fulfill their poultry-raising needs, most especially chicken feed. I remember as a child going down to the farm-and-ranch store in my hometown on Saturdays with my father. I don't know why we went there, as we lived in a normal city neighborhood and didn't have livestock or chickens. Perhaps my dad was buying lawn fertilizer, but I do remember that I always looked forward to going with him. I remember most the specific odor of the dark, dusty place. It was a warm, pleasant amalgam that my memory tells me was a mixture of penned animals (specifically chickens and rabbits), sawdust, leather horse tack, Purina feed, and the sharp, acrid scent of fertilizer.

Those memories came flooding back when I went into the Urban Farm Store in Southeast Portland last summer, but the similarities to the feed store we patronized back in Abilene pretty much end there. The Urban Farm Store updates the old-fashioned farm-and-feed in a very Portland sort of way. Robert Litt, its owner with the requisite baseball hat and beard of an urban hipster, opened the business after 10 years of being a landscape architect. The recently expanded operation sells several kinds of baby chicks, heirloom open-pollinated seeds, local organic feed, fruit trees, and vegetable and herb seedlings to a loyal clientele from the surrounding downtown neighborhoods of historic bungalows surrounded by small gardens.

Robert Litt, *above,* opened his Urban Farm Store to accommodate a growing number of backyard chicken enthusiasts in Portland, Oregon.

While I was there, the phone rang every few minutes with a question from a concerned urban farmer, or a young mom would come in with a baby stroller to buy chicken feed. The store is designed to be a center for the community, offering classes in raising chickens, gardening, and even home butchering for those ready to embrace the full urban food-growing experience.

Litt and his wife, Hannah, keep a variety of poultry at their Portland backyard and maintain an extensive vegetable garden. Through his own experiences raising chickens and from what he hears and sees from customers, he feels that the craze may be peaking, but that once the wave recedes, there will still be a dedicated group of people who want to keep poultry at home. He admits that he sees two kinds of chicken keepers: urban farmers, who he thinks will continue the practice, and those people who transfer their chickens to pet status. He surmises that some of the latter group will not be able to handle the more challenging aspects of chickens: their sometimes yucky diseases and the maintenance involved with keeping up the coops. "It's also important to remember that the birds have a relatively short life span," he adds for those people looking for a long-term relationship. But the community building continues as his customers repeatedly come to his store for their organic, locally sourced feed and a little free chicken-rearing advice.

In addition to their chickens, Robert and Hannah Litt tend an extensive garden of vegetables and fruits at their Portland backyard.

Local Regulations

Check your local government's zoning code to be sure that raising chickens and tending bees are permitted where you live (start by searching online first). Most municipalities have restrictions on the number of chickens that you can keep, and many forbid noisy roosters for the sake of neighborhood harmony. In addition, city officials have historically been inordinately frightened of honeybees. However, more and more communities seem to be relaxing their laws. For example, New York City recently allowed urban beekeeping—to the thrill of locavores citywide.

CHAPTER 11
Shared Spaces

I'VE HAD A SOFT SPOT FOR COMMUNITY GARDENS ever since I moved to New York City in the late 1980s. During my first year, I lived in a small studio apartment in the once gritty far western edge of Chelsea. I was fairly starved for green leaves and flowers, so I often altered my route from my home to walk by the community plots and public gardens around the city. Most of our public gardens were old-fashioned parks and squares with trees, lawns, and benches. Bette Midler (and others) had not yet set her formidable sights on renovating the many neglected parks in forgotten corners of the city. But an intriguing few were of the "Hey, let's put on a show!" sort founded by urban activism groups such as the Green Guerillas, who first tilled miraculous gardens out of neglected lots in the 1970s. The scrappy, can-do attitude of these grassroots movements was the source of real change to the city's open spaces.

Green Pioneers

One of my early favorite sites to visit was the LaGuardia Corner Gardens next to a supermarket in Greenwich Village. Through the chain link, I could see orderly plots of perennials and flowering shrubs being tended by their owners well past twilight. I loved to go there after dinner to smell the moonflowers along the inordinately tall fence—perhaps a leftover

More often than not, city dwellers don't have their own private spaces to garden and grow food. Shared gardens, like the Colonel Summers community garden in Portland, *above*, successfully fill the gap.

Run by farmer Annie Novak, the Eagle Street Rooftop Farm in Greenpoint, Brooklyn, produces food for its own market days and also functions as a teaching space for local schoolchildren.

from a more challenging time security-wise. I also often walked down Greenwich Avenue to see what was blooming behind the dignified iron gates of the Jefferson Market Garden or stopped on my way across East Houston to peer into the deep shade created by the gigantic dawn redwood at the Liz Christy Garden—the first community garden in New York City. Even though I never stuck my hand in their soil, these gardens provided my initial exposure to urban gardens. I'll admit that I was a bit of a benign stalker, watching carefully from afar but too shy to chat with the busy gardeners. All these years later, I am less shy. While checking out the various garden scenes across the United States for this book, I got my chance to speak to some of the country's most exciting community-oriented gardeners and witness what they've created, and I found out that I still still deeply admire the democracy of these places. In our crowded cities, not everyone is lucky enough to have his or her own piece of land to grow things. That's why shared gardens have become important as our population increases. People who live in apartments, rentals, or multifamily buildings need space to garden, too. What better use could there be for a disused or neglected piece of land than to have someone love it?

A Farm in the Sky

One such example, not a proper community garden per se, can be found sited improbably on a rooftop at the northern industrial edges of Brooklyn. The 6,000-square-foot space is three floors above the quiet streets of Greenpoint, a primarily working-class neighborhood that borders trendy Williamsburg on

Judging by the good health of the crops like cauliflower and tomatoes, *below*, tended by an experienced farmer like Annie Novak and her group of volunteers, you wouldn't know the farm is three stories up.

Find Out More about Supporting Local Farming

- The Center for Food Safety (http://truefoodnow. org). Monitors food sources and production.

- Civil Eats (http://civileats.com). Critical thoughts on sustainable food systems.

- Community Alliance with Family Farmers (www.caff.org). Promotes small-scale farming practices.

- Just Food (www.justfood.org). Connects area farms to neighborhoods in New York City.

- Local Harvest (www.localharvest.org). Find greenmarkets in your area.

- Slow Food USA (www.slowfoodusa.org). Supports and preserves American food traditions.

its south side and is bounded by the East River and, on the north, the borough of Queens and the exceptionally polluted Newtown Creek. Annie Novak and Ben Flanner, both residents of Brooklyn, started the rooftop farm project after the two met while searching for a way to do an urban agriculture project. Flanner approached Eric and Lisa Goode of the green roof specialists Goode Green Design for help in figuring out how to make a productive organic farm on a rooftop somewhere in the city. Flanner, a first-time farmer, soon enlisted Novak because she had gained agricultural experience farming at a variety of projects overseas over the past several years. The Goodes—who have worked in the film business—found a space owned by Gina Argento and her family, whose company Broadway Stages operates a number of soundstages around Brooklyn and Long Island City. The Argentos became

the benefactors of the project, donating a rooftop space on one of their buildings and funding the installation and design. The Goodes called on the technological and structural expertise that they have gathered over the past years of doing rooftop gardens to create the elevated growing space where once there was just a dead zone of roofing material. With these connections, Novak and Flanner were able to accomplish the seemingly impossible: an impressively productive organic farm where tomatoes, eggplants, tomatillos, peppers, chard, melons, and beans are grown in 4 to 7 inches of soil on a roof with panoramic river views of the Manhattan skyline.

The farm has gotten a lot of media attention; visiting magazine reporters and foreign film crews are a semiregular sight on the rooftop. "Everything has come hurricane fast," Novak says. But aside from the distractions of all this attention, the windy aboveground site has its more natural challenges. Certain plants like winter squash and broccoli never seemed to adapt, but tomatoes thrived even as other East Coast gardeners found their potential harvest succumbing to late blight. Novak, who is a coordinator of programming for children at the Howell Family Garden at the New York Botanical Garden and a former farmers' aide with the city's greenmarket program, helped lay out the planting design, organizing dozens of varieties of vegetables in 16 four-foot-wide east–west facing rows (two more face north and south) in free-draining soil that had been enriched with mushroom compost. Obviously, the setup costs are high to put an astounding 200,000 pounds of soil on the roof, but as Novak says, "once all that stuff is up there, it's up there."

From April through October, the farmers and their volunteer helpers, an eager group of city dwellers only too happy to get their hands in the "ground" and experience the concept of truly local food, work the soil and harvest produce for the farm's on-site Sunday market. Next year, Novak hopes to hire two full-time farmers as the enterprise becomes more commercially viable. The hours are hard and long, but it's easy to imagine the thrill of being surrounded by miles of buildings at dawn as the sun shines into the enormous mirrored facades and canyonlike streets of Midtown Manhattan, illuminating the tugboats and sailboats on the river.

Novak, who lives 4 blocks from the farm, says one of her main interests is to pursue urban farming as a community builder. "We started by selling our produce to local restaurants, but I somehow like the direct sale to the public more," she says. "I like connecting people to their food. That resonates with me." She hopes to expand the local impact and educational aspects of the Eagle Street Rooftop Farm, as it is now called, by bringing in more school groups to see the growing space and launching a CSA (community-supported agriculture) pickup spot where customers can subscribe to receive a portion of what she grows. In what would seem her exceedingly slim spare time, Novak also started Growing Chefs (http://growingchefs.org), an organization that teaches kids how to grow and cook fresh produce. The rooftop farm trend is spreading; Flanner recently branched out to start another large top-story farm elsewhere in Queens. In the future, wouldn't it be magnificent to fly in to land at one of the nearby airports and see acres of rooftop gardens and farms where before there was only tar paper and reflective roof paint?

Food Justice Grows in Chicago

Even though Erika Allen grew up on her family's Wisconsin farm, it took a roundabout path through an art degree from the Art Institute of Chicago for her to come back to help in the family business. She was raised working on the farm outside of Milwaukee doing real labor, not just chores, so she had

little interest in continuing down that hard-worn path in the beginning of her adult life. But the influence of her charismatic father, Will Allen, who was once a former professional basketball player, would change all that. "My father told me, 'You'll thank me one day. You'll know how to grow food and other people won't,'" she remembers. The senior Allen has become something of a celebrity in urban agriculture circles and a 2008 MacArthur Fellow to boot. The motto of Growing Power, the Milwaukee-based nonprofit that he founded, is: "Inspiring communities to build sustainable food systems that are equitable and ecologically sound, creating a just world, one food-secure community at a time." He farms on several sites around Milwaukee, where he runs a variety of productive greenhouses filled with various salad greens, sprouts, and other vegetables; fisheries of tilapia and yellow perch; beehives; worm depositories; and poultry and livestock pens, where he teaches programs on integrated sustainable growing practices, food distribution, and soil enrichment.

"During the events of 9/11," Erika Allen says, "I was working at a social service food pantry and I started thinking, what would happen if we didn't grow any of our food anymore at all and something really terrible happened? We need a decentralized food system." Soon her interest in social justice and food policy drew her back to join the family business, and she launched a satellite operation in Chicago that maintains several community gardens and educational programs that focus on getting young people interested in growing food. "So few of them know anything about it," she says.

Maybe conventional in-ground farms are more practical but Eagle Street Rooftop Farm is a model publicity machine for the concept of local food growing. Annie Novak, *opposite*, harvests Italian chicory at her rooftop farm. Baby radishes poke out of the shallow, free-draining soil mix.

Erika Allen, *opposite*, runs the Chicago branch of Growing Power, a community-based agriculture program that turns public space like Grant Park, *above and below*, into beautiful and productive gardens.

Art on the Farm
urban agriculture "potager" kitchen garden

The most visible of Growing Power's projects is the Art on the Farm Urban Agriculture Potager in downtown Chicago's Grant Park. What at first glance appears to be traditional symmetric municipal beds of annual flowers, very much in keeping with the historic plan designed for the city's lakefront, turns out to be edible and organic. The potager contains 20,000 square feet of beds on 2 acres, which Allen designed for Moore Landscapes under the auspices of Adam Schwerner, the Chicago Park District's director of the department of natural resources. The farm trains interns from educational youth programs, and the youngsters learn about food sources, culinary variety, and horticulture and tend over 150 varieties of vegetables, edible flowers, and herbs. The resulting produce is sold at area farmers' markets and restaurants, given away to food programs, or eaten by the interns during demonstration meals. Most of the plants fare pretty well in a location that is exposed to both the ravages of the lakeside elements and the general public. On my early morning visit, I noticed a woman blithely walking away with few handfuls of salad greens. When I asked Allen about what I had seen, she said that the occasional light-fingered pedestrian doesn't worry her too much. When the garden lost much of its first tomato crop, however, she switched to tomatoes with more unusual colors, like 'Green Zebra'. The sneaky fruit throws off potential thieves because it never appears to ripen (even though it does, and deliciously so).

Growing Power, with projects including community allotments and teaching centers at Jackson Park and Cabrini-Green, continues to expand its mission in Chicago through several other sites for urban farms. Here, Allen expands her mission to reconnect urban citizens with their food, especially those who live in areas underserved by commercial supermarkets, where even the simplest community garden becomes a powerful civilizing agent. Allen, who is a well-

spoken advocate for her endeavors, credits the progressive scene in Chicago to a loose group of organizations including Growing Home, which trains the homeless in green jobs; City Farms, which turns neglected lots into profitable vegetable plots; and the Bee Line and the Chicago Honey Co-op, which craft honey and beeswax beauty products from urban harvested hives. She says that without these groups and their larger umbrella group, the Chicago Food Policy Advisory Council (www.chicagofoodpolicy.org), there would be many more barriers to urban agriculture in Chicago. "There are a lot of politics in the art world, but nothing like this," she says.

Granted, the cities of the rust belt have their share of vacant lots. But they also have a long tradition of community activism that stretches from Jane Addams and Florence Kelley's efforts with the burgeoning immigrant community in the 19th century to more recent projects on the South Side.

For both Allens, it's not just about remaking empty properties and corners of parks into vegetable gardens. They have made a lot of progress with their own self-sufficiency; the business has 38 full-time employees in Milwaukee and four full-time employees in Chicago. But there is a long way to go to realize the Allens' dream of full community self-sufficiency for urban gardeners. The key is to create jobs and a sustainable business model that provides meaningful amounts of food for a population that has been neglected by America's centralized food system.

For the gardener interested in public horticulture, a visit to Chicago is inspirational on many levels. Most visibly there is Millennium Park, which is a model for all future urban open spaces thanks to the almost childlike wonder of its interactive artwork, forward-thinking design, and naturalistic plantings—all on a giant green roof above an underground

On Chicago's South Side, the Gary Comer Youth Center features an educational roof garden of edible plants, *above*, tended by volunteers and local schoolchildren.

End and a native of the neighborhood, funded the award-winning, $30 million building designed by architect John Ronan. Its most obviously unusual feature is the colorful tile-clad exterior. Inside, the center provides extracurricular activities and classes for more than 600 kids from one of Chicago's poorest neighborhoods. Last season, its unexpectedly modern roof garden yielded 1,000 pounds of produce, including lettuce, collard and mustard greens, kale, strawberries, okra, squash, peas, and herbs from a soil depth of 12 to 18 inches spread out over the 8,600 square feet.

Peter Schaudt of Hoerr Schaudt Landscape Architects, who designed the green roof planting system, says that one of the challenges of the project was its extreme setting: the harsh exposure, sun, and wind of the site, even though it is surrounded like a courtyard by the windows of the staff offices. Also, the membrane and watering systems had to be strong enough to withstand the traffic and sometimes overly enthusiastic digging of the young student gardeners. The depth of the soil added greatly to the project costs, since the building had to be strengthened to support the soil weight, but all the participants—especially Gary Comer, who passed away from cancer shortly after the opening of the center in 2006—did not want to turn back. The extra soil depth allows for certain kinds of plants that would struggle in a thinner layer of soil. As examples, Schaudt mentions the big waving stands of perennial grasses and the carrots that grow long before comically turning 90 degrees when they hit the roof membrane.

Marjorie Hess, the garden's manager, feels that her main goals are to get her students interested in food, both how it's grown and how it is prepared, and to create a sense

parking garage. But far away from the skyscrapers, there are equally fascinating community-centered projects in parts of town where tourists don't normally go, such as the city's South Side. Surrounded by empty lots of weedy concrete and low-rise housing in a once thriving but now neglected neighborhood called Greater Grand Crossing, a modernist vegetable garden sits hidden on top of the Gary Comer Youth Center. Comer, the late founder of catalog retailer Lands'

of separation from some of the harsh daily realities of their lives. To accomplish this, she incorporates flowering perennials and grass with the edible plants so that the roof has the wild sense of a meadow. She says that many of the students are not used to being outdoors in a place where they can feel completely safe while they go about their summer school programs, math lessons, and art and cooking classes. Cherish Solomon, a then 12-year-old student of the center, said it best when she was quoted in an article in the *Chicago Tribune* in 2008: "The garden makes me feel poetic . . . . The soil is soft. The flowers, when they bloom, it's beautiful. It makes me feel relaxed. Coming up to the rooftop . . . it makes my mind explode. I feel like I'm laying out on a cloud." The garden also receives twice-a-week visits from some of the neighborhood's senior citizen population, who come by to garden and impart wisdom gained from years of experience. On the day of my visit, I met a gardener who was over 100 years old, and though she might have not gotten down on her hands and knees to tend the plants, she certainly knew how to best grow vegetables in the city.

Opposite: Narrow beds and lots of walkways make access easy for the students at the Gary Comer Youth Center. *Above:* Under the auspices of a nonprofit environmental education organization called the Resource Center, City Farm has taken over a previously vacant pie-shaped wedge next to the last undemolished buildings of the Cabrini-Green public housing development on Chicago's North Side. A thick layer of composted soil was added over the top. Volunteers from the surrounding neighborhood sell the produce on-site and to chefs around town. Once the lot is sold, the farm will relocate to another underused spot and start again.

Urban Apiary

Chicago beekeeper Michael Thompson keeps dozens of hives on the site of a former industrial parking lot for Sears, Roebuck and Co. in the North Lawndale neighborhood. The thousands of bees of the Chicago Honey Co-op find nectar in nearby linden trees, white sweet clover, aster, goldenrod, and other weeds and wildflowers that are reclaiming the many vacant lots of the surrounding residential neighborhood. Thompson and his employees tend the hives and gather the honey that is sold as its delectable sweet self or used in a variety of beauty products available at greenmarkets or through mail order (www.chicagohoneycoop.com).

Collective Gardening

In my estimation, the only urban area that rivals Chicago for its progressive, civic-minded horticulture is Portland, Oregon. The city seems to have the concept of community gardens down to a science. The fenced plot at Colonel Summers Park in Southeast Portland is one of the most floriferous and vegetable-filled examples I've ever seen. Dan Franek, the botanical specialist for Portland's community garden program, says that the Colonel Summers garden is the most popular in the city, with a waiting list of over 100 people (the turnover rate he estimates to be 8 or 9 years). Not a day goes by, he says, where he doesn't take a call from someone asking to sign up for this particular location, even though there are 32 other community gardens in the city—and more on the way.

Certainly, the space has the funky, laid-back energy that most garden cooperatives have, and its disparate structures made of wire, wood, plastic, rubber, metal, and string give it a somewhat chaotic appearance—but that is what makes it so special. Community gardens keep things real and authentic by necessity instead of design. Space has to be optimized. Materials are often recycled rather ingeniously. One gardener's junk might turn out to be a problem-solver for her neighbor. There is a collective feeling of a sum that is greater than its parts, like a graceful jellyfish made up of many individuals acting for the common good.

How to Find a Community Garden near You

American Community Garden Association (www.communitygarden.org): Browse a clickable map to find places to garden near you, with contact information and short descriptions.

Though they rarely make a cohesive design statement, community gardens such as the one at Colonel Summers Park in Portland display lots of idiosyncratic charm, like this inventive raised bed system, *opposite top*, and ladder-cum-trellis, *below*. I find the inspiring spirit of collectivism very appealing.

Gardening for the Good

One of the most successful components of gardening occurs when someone takes the idea of growing plants and attaches it to a cause. For Growing Gardens, a nonprofit in Portland, the idea is to get people who might not ordinarily garden into their yards to grow food. On my visit, Rodney Bender, the organization's program manager, took me to Northeast Portland to visit Teri Phillips. In a narrow lampchop-shaped garden outside her duplex, Phillips—who sustains some of the debilitating aftereffects of childhood polio—showed me her vegetable-filled yard with bashfully nervous pride. Almost every square foot was used to grow things. The Growing Gardens program installs raised planters in, as the Web site says, "backyards, front yards, side yards, and even on balconies." These wooden box gardens are then filled with soil and compost, and the recipients are taught organic growing practices and supported with advice, seedlings, and horticultural assistance for a period of 3 years. The group also gives workshops in how to cook and preserve the produce so that nothing goes to waste.

A participant of the program for several years, Phillips is the picture of rosy good health except for the aid of her cane. During the sunny growing season, she spends her days more outdoors than inside, as she keeps busy around the yard, harvesting baskets of peas and checking on the progress of a line of corn that backs the trellised pea vines. Next to small patch of lawn where Phillips can sit out of the sun and take a break stands a thicket of Jerusalem artichokes, garlic, and berry bushes—all packed efficiently in what seems less than 500 square feet of ornamental productivity.

Teri Phillips' pole beans form a tall green fence along the street next to her driveway full of boxes filled with rainbow chard, peppers, and tomatoes.

CHAPTER 12

Gardening the Street

SOME OF OUR most obvious and public garden spaces are also some of our most often overlooked. Street-side gardening can open up a neighborhood and get people outside and engaged with one another in a way that a row of wall-like hedges and houses with setback garages never will. This is especially true in inner-city neighborhoods, where often just a few years back crime, drugs, and a general feeling of

despair seemed facts of urban life. People actively tending their gardens and the surrounding street tree beds usually leads to the formation of block associations, which in turn leads to crime watch programs and less criminal activity. As seen in some of the tougher sections of our cities, nothing deters crime like a group of gardeners working in their front yards days and evenings with one eye firmly on the tasks at hand and the other on any suspicious characters.

The Greenest Block

Since 1994, the Brooklyn Botanic Garden's Greenest Block in Brooklyn Contest has awarded such endeavors. Lincoln Road, a beautiful tree-lined street with landmarked bow-front limestone houses in the Lefferts Gardens area, was a first-time winner in 2009 (full disclosure: I was a judge in the contest). This particular street, like other parts of brownstone Brooklyn with its million-dollar single-family houses, doesn't now

In many cities, gardening the sidewalk strip is discouraged. Two communities—Portland, Oregon, *opposite*, and Venice, California, *above*—have taken the practice of street-front gardening nearly to an art form.

seem like a much of a haven for criminal activity, but not long ago things were more challenging. The current strength of these neighborhoods comes not merely from an influx of new, often wealthier, residents moving in to rejuvenate properties that were neglected or abandoned by former residents as different waves of immigration moved through. That narrative oversimplifies the stories of these constantly evolving neighborhoods. Instead, solid middle-class streets like Lincoln Road have been quietly racially integrated for decades—and happily so. They only get stronger as newcomers and old-timers alike join forces in block associations. Tolonda Tolbert currently leads the Lincoln Road organization as its president. A resident of the street for the past 7 years since she moved from the East Village, the Colorado native works with a dedicated team of neighbors to encourage gardening participation among the block's 80 homes. "With the block association, there is a coordinated approach to how we garden the street," Tolbert says. "It's not just about your own yard. We want everyone's place to look good." These days, the block is a showcase for urban horticulture and cooperation, with 80 percent taking part.

During the sultry Brooklyn summers, the front yards overflow with lilac butterfly bushes and magenta crape myrtles; fragrant passionflowers and honeysuckle vines run rampant on wrought-iron gates. Longer-term or older residents pass on their horticultural techniques and plant knowledge to newer homeowners. But as in any good team, it's hard to say who's responsible for what. Tolbert says that the aim is to get people to think beyond their own yards and about the block as a whole. Many of the plants—dahlias, four o'clocks, and hostas—are traded back and forth, along with seeds of prized varieties. "We rarely buy a plant," Tolbert says. Over time, the resulting consistency of the street's plant palette makes it seem like one long contiguous garden. Younger residents pitch in to help the older gardeners who once loved to work in their yards but can no longer perform the necessary physical labor. Another

Block association president Tolanda Tolbert, *opposite*, is justifiably proud of her street's recent win as Greenest Block in Brooklyn. She describes the street gardening on her block as a group effort of neighbor helping neighbor, formed of both newcomers and old-timers.

important contribution of the new streetscape are the curbside gardens, where residents have removed the large broken or concrete squares next to the road that go unrepaired by the city, replacing them with flower-filled gardens that help absorb some of the rainfall before it goes to waste in the gutter.

Tolbert, a diversity consultant for educational institutions and nonprofits, loves living on this block with her husband and children. She is working on a film project in which the neighborhood teenagers interview the septuagenarians and octogenarians about the area's integration over the past 50 years. She reports that the association is thriving and thrilled with their award. "As a newcomer, I can't take any credit for the recent gardening honor—I'm just a spokesperson," she says. "We do it because we love flowers. And to get recognition for all our hard work is an added bonus." Tolbert, who had never gardened at all before moving to Lincoln Road, is learning everything she can from the more experienced gardening residents about plant propagation and transplanting. Though there are still a few houses on Lincoln Road that remain conspicuously bare and ungardened, the drive of this block association to help unify its diverse neighborhood on the eastern edge of Prospect Park is a model that can be replicated in cities across the country. Such informal movements and programs could especially be beneficial in areas like Detroit, where foreclosures have decimated neighborhoods and threaten to make once thriving communities into urban ghost towns.

A Yard-Sharing Utopia

Before visiting Portland, Oregon, for the first time, I had heard a lot about its dark, wet winters and earnest liberal politics. But I wasn't there for the bleak months, so I had the chance to see the city in its sunniest disposition. Each day was clear, warm, and so blue that it felt like paradise. Countless people pedaled by on bicycles, and the streets were filled with gardening activity. The population seemed young and happy, and they were eager to tell me how much they loved their town. But when asked about the winters, each person would visibly sink a little and sigh, "Oh yeah, the winters . . ." Everyone I talked to, no matter how long they had lived in Portland, said something along those lines. I think this period of darkness and indoor isolation makes the people of Portland want to celebrate their bright summer months by taking to the streets to garden en masse—when they're not on their bicycles, that is.

I have never seen such a high level of community-oriented horticulture as I did in that city. Growing organic food there is a big deal, as it would be in any place with this number of hip 20- and 30-year-olds. People are planting edibles all over town, in conventional community gardens (some of the nicest and most well-loved of any I've seen) and, more surprisingly, right out in their front yards in what once was lawn. In a practice called yard sharing, several houses in a row take out their lawns, and each property grows a different set of vegetables or fruit, then the harvest gets divided among the participants. It's a good way for the small-scale gardener to deal with the inevitable zucchini surplus without resorting to weeks of ratatouille. On a deeper level, yard sharing knits these communities together in an inspiring way.

Yard sharing isn't only for people in contiguous properties who would like to link up. It also connects apartment dwellers and people with yards that aren't suitable for horticulture with occupants of single-family homes who would like someone to use their space for growing food. There's even a Web site, www.yardsharing.org, started by Joshua Patterson, a Portland resident who heard about the 1,000-plus

Lawnless yards and imaginatively gardened sidewalk strips like this forest of sunflowers distinguish much of Portland's streetscapes, *opposite.*

people around the city who are on waiting lists for much-sought-after community garden space. He wanted to find a way to link people who have unused yard space and a desire for homegrown food with those gardeners looking for a plot to tend. As one ad on the Web site stated: "We are looking for a sunny plot to grow vegetables, as our small yard is primarily shade. Will share our veggies with you. Thanks!"

This shared approach to gardening makes Portland feel like a very welcoming city. Walking around the neighborhood of Southeast Portland, with its dozens and dozens of blocks of bungalows and cottages, it's easy to feel that the citizens want their gardens to be appreciated by everyone—they don't want the limitations and sequestration of tall fences or hedges. This is gardening as performance art, with each yard trying to make its own statement. Some yards take a more-is-more approach and fill their yards with glorious thickets of perennials and shrubs. Design is not always the paramount motivation. There are fewer examples of the high-style architect-driven house-and-garden renovations as you might see in Los Angeles or San Francisco. These yards have a grassroots, homegrown feel that is reassuringly and resolutely old-fashioned. And during our recent boom years of rapid gentrification and homogenization of building styles across the country, this stubborn refusal to fancy things up becomes a political statement in itself.

A vital street gardening scene makes parts of Portland into perhaps American's largest community garden. Public art projects, sidewalk plantings, and shared yards are common sights in artsy bungalow neighborhoods like Southwest Portland.

Yard Sharing in Other Areas

GardenSwap
(http://gardenswap.org):
Los Angeles

Hyperlocavore
(http://hyperlocavore.ning.com):
United States

Sharing Backyards
(www.sharingbackyards.com):
United States and international

Urban Gardenshare
(www.urbangardenshare.org):
Seattle

Yards to Gardens
(www.y2g.org):
Minneapolis–St. Paul

Portland's front-yard planting styles range from urban meadows to shared vegetable plots to rock gardens. It's difficult to find an old-fashioned mown front lawn in certain parts of town.

An edible thicket of artichokes and elderberries swallows a Portland sidewalk.

As front yards of clipped lawns and orderly flowerbeds become harder to find in Portland, so do ordinary barren sidewalk plantings. The no-man's-land that lies between the concrete sidewalk and asphalt street appears destined to be an unresolved space in most cities and towns. No one can even agree on a good name for it. The British-sounding *verge* is my preference, since it's short, but there are other options: *tree lawn, sidewalk buffer, nature strip, utility easement, planting strip, parkway, devil strip,* and the ever-popular *hell strip.* The legality of gardening the verge in front of your own house is often unclear, because the city owns and maintains the areas in many communities. But in freethinking Portland, the verge is fair game. In one neighborhood, for example, some folks installed raised wooden planters of vegetables and herbs, others created tall sidewalk jungles of sunflowers or artichokes, while someone else in the house next door made a more restrained statement with a meadow of yarrow, nepeta, and ornamental grass. It is important to consider several things when gardening the sidewalk verge. Try to use plants that are drought tolerant, since the area usually is unconnected to any supplemental irrigation. And if you live in areas with hard winters, you'll want to select species that can take the salt spray or whatever chemical nastiness the highway department will be using to keep the roads free of ice.

Planting the Verge in Venice

Gardening the sidewalk strip has almost become an art form in Venice, California. All over its seaside blocks, homeowners are annexing the unplanted verges next to the street. Tall cacti, ornamental grasses, and subtropical shrubs like pineapple guavas (*Feijoa sellowiana*) or grassy phormiums create leafy tunnels for pedestrians to walk through. Like Portland, Venice is a community with a tradition of alternative thinking, so each front garden appears as individualistic as its owner. Curbside plantings become galleries displaying a range of styles and approaches. Some reveal the hand of a professional designer with a restrictive palette of plants in disciplined and tasteful color schemes. Other verge gardens, the work of passionate amateurs, showcase many kinds of plants arranged in a glorious sort of chaos that can be exhilarating to experience on a neighborhood walk.

The Gowanus Garden Lady

We gardeners sometimes end up in the oddest places. New Hampshire native Kirstin Tobiasson never thought she'd live in New York City, much less in the gritty industrial neighborhood surrounding Brooklyn's Gowanus Canal. These days, the neighborhood is known for two main things: its trendy area of artists' lofts mixed with some of the last vestiges of light manufacturing in Brooklyn, and its historic but disused and intensely polluted shipping canal that leads out to New York Harbor. In 2002 in this unlikely spot, Tobiasson created a small streetside garden on a former dumping ground for every bad thing a big city has to offer: decades' worth of garbage, dog poop, syringes, crack vials, old condoms, and discarded pieces of concrete. Originally, she had a studio in the warehouse behind the garden (she since has moved to an apartment 7 blocks away). "Something made me look down from the fire escape at the plots of bare earth, and I thought I should make a garden there," she says.

Tobiasson had never gardened before. But with the help of a neighbor, she started digging up the big chunks of broken concrete that littered the area. Not knowing where to dispose of them, she stacked the concrete like stones to form raised beds that she then filled with new soil. "I hardly spent any money," she says. "I got my initial plants from my mom, who is a great gardener, and free compost from the city's giveaway program." She then only had to buy the additional soil from the garden center. Her garden started with a small, 8- by 10-foot patch, but Tobiasson quickly expanded the beds to fill any empty earth that she

Above and overleaf: Over the past several years, Kirstin Tobiasson has carved out a renegade slice of gardening paradise near the industrial Gowanus Canal in Brooklyn, *opposite.* Along the way, she learned a lot about the unyielding vagaries of urban horticulture and city politics. Her self-seeded sunflowers and hand-me-down or donated plants thrive just steps from the polluted canal, a newly designated Superfund site.

could find, including a 3- by 25-foot strip next to the street. She favors bright flowers like the clumps of golden glow (*Rudbeckia laciniata* 'Hortensia') that her mother gave her, which still thrives in the garden. She also plants marigolds, nasturtiums, alyssum, bee balm, and sunflowers that can compete with the visual distraction of her urban location right next to the canal and the Union Street drawbridge. As her garden grew, she began to get more and more attention from pedestrians and bicyclists, who today still leave her thank-you notes and gifts of seed packets. "People stop and tell me how the garden has changed their way of thinking about their neighborhood," she says. "Or they tell me how they've changed their route to work so that they can come by and watch the garden grow." Children referred to her as the Garden Lady.

The attention was encouraging, but then she realized that she hadn't ever asked the landlord, who doesn't come around much, about the garden. Although he stopped by about 2 years into the project and gave her his blessing, it turned out that the terms of his insurance required that the streetside beds be cemented over. Tobiasson was shocked to learn that part of her precious garden was going to be dismantled. After months of trying to reason with the city, Tobiasson relocated the plantings from her long streetside beds to make way for a bleak new concrete sidewalk. "I realized I just couldn't fight the city," she says. "It's a difficult thing to get permission for this sort of thing." At one point an official wanted to charge Tobiasson for the privilege of gardening the remaining abandoned plots, even though the city had left them empty and derelict for many years.

Despite the regulatory dramas, the garden has been a hands-on education for Tobiasson. It has encouraged her to earn a certificate in horticulture from the Brooklyn Botanic Garden and to get a job with a local landscape design company. As she continues her education, she realizes that her

little garden requires too much water, and she is adjusting her plantings accordingly by including low-water species that can handle the garden's south-facing summer heat. She says she's never spent more than $250 on the garden; everything except mulch and soil amendments comes mostly as freebies and gifts. "I've never approached this garden with a clean-palette, full-wallet mentality," Tobiasson says. "But now, it's got to take care of itself a little better without me."

Even with its reduced size, Tobiasson's garden is a benefit to the neighborhood and—in its small way—to the health of the canal that was designated recently with great controversy as an EPA Superfund cleanup site. Ironically, her struggles coincided with a plea from New York City's Mayor Bloomberg for greater areas of permeability around the city to combat the city's problems with its old-fashioned combined sewer overflow (CSO) system. It's a 19th-century system ineffectively servicing a 21st-century city: Every time a large storm comes through New York City, rainwater from gutters gets mixed in with raw sewage, which in turn overwhelms the processing plants. The untreated pathogenic overflow then goes straight into major rivers and canals like the Gowanus. An island city like New York is crying out for professionally designed storm-water gardens like the government-funded projects that can be seen in Portland. Combine these with scores of renegade plots like Tobiasson's garden, and a significant amount of rainfall could be absorbed and kept out of our precious waterways.

Commuting pedestrians and bicyclists seem to appreciate Kirstin Tobiasson's gardening efforts. They leave little gifts and notes of thanks, proof that gardens create community in even the most unlikely places where industrial concerns and pollution once set the tone of the neighborhood.

Resources

Featured Garden Designers and Landscape Architects

Carolyn Doepke Bennett
cdb gardens
323-632-9200
carolyn@cdbgardens.com

Barry Campion
Campion Walker Garden Design, Inc.
1044 Palms Boulevard
Venice, CA 90291
310-392-3535
barry@campionwalker.com
www.campionwalker.com

James David
David/Peese Design
8 Sugar Creek
Austin, TX 78746
512-327-9324
www.davidpeesedesign.com

Emmanuel Donval
Green Cherry Landscape
Architecture
1336 Calistoga Avenue
Napa, CA 94559
415-548-4711
emmanueldonval@gmail.com
www.greencherry.biz

Amy Falder and Chris Brunner
New York Green Roofs, LLC
72 Bedford, Suite 6A
New York, NY 10014
917-680-6881
info@redefinetheskyline.com
www.redefinetheskyline.com

Goode Green
Green Roof Design and Installation
176 Grand Street, Office 602
New York, NY 10013
212-226-6770
info@goodegreennyc.com
www.goodegreennyc.com

Jay Griffith
717 California Avenue
Venice, CA 90291
310-392-5558
www.jaygriffith.com

Flora Grubb Gardens
1634 Jerrold Avenue
San Francisco CA 94110
415-648-2670
www.floragrubb.com

Berthold Haas
Berthold Haas Design
618 Lavaca, Suite 11
Austin, TX 78701
512-236-9645
www.bertholdhaasdesign.com

Nathaniel Harris and Emma de Caires
Blue Dahlia Gardens
info@bdgardens.com
www.bdgardens.com

Paul Hendershot Design, Inc.
353 Old Baldwin Road
Ojai, CA 93023
805-646-7199
www.paulhendershotdesign.com

Hoerr Schaudt Landscape Architects
850 West Jackson Boulevard
Suite 800
Chicago, Illinois 60607
312-492-6501
info@hoerrschaudt.com
www.hoerrschaudt.com

Judy M. Horton
136½ N. Larchmont Boulevard,
Suite B
Los Angeles, CA 90004
323-462-1413
jhorton@jmhgardendesign.com

Julie Jordin
The Garden Design Company
PO Box 3153
Nantucket, MA 02584
508-325-4080
julie@juliejordin.com
http://juliejordin.com

Judy Kameon
Elysian Landscapes
2340 W. Third Street
Los Angeles CA 90057
213-380-3185
info@elysianlandscapes.com
www.elysianlandscapes.com

Patrick Kirwin
Kirwin Horticultural Services, LLC
408 Valley
San Marcos, TX 78666
512-878-8903
www.khsgardendesigns.com

Sean Knibb
Knibb Design
1522 Abbot Kinney
Venice, CA 90291
310-450-5552
info@knibbdesign.com
www.knibbdesign.com

Robert Leeper
Robert Leeper Landscapes
512-751-4642
www.RobertLeeperDesigns.com

James Lord and Roderick Wyllie
Surfacedesign Inc.
131 Lower Terrace
San Francisco, CA 94114
415-621-5522
info@sdisf.com
www.sdisf.com

Beth Mullins
Growsgreen Landscape Design
415-336-9829
beth@growsgreen.com
www.growsgreen.com

Jeff Pervorse
Bent Grass
618 Westminster Avenue, #3
Venice, CA 90291
310-399-6522
jeff@bent-grass.com
www.bent-grass.com

Dylan Robertson
D-Crain Landscape Design and
Construction
1621 Willow Street
Austin, TX 78702
512-480-8008
studio@d-crain.com
www.d-crain.com

Christy Ten Eyck, FASLA
Ten Eyck Landscape Architects, Inc.
2506 Bridle Path
Austin, TX 78703
512-492-5808
teneyck@teneyckla.com
www.teneyckla.com

Mark Tessier
Mark Tessier Landscape
Architecture
1424 4th Street, Suite 234
Santa Monica, CA 90401
310-395-3595
info@marktessier.com
www.marktessier.com

Bernard Trainor
Bernard Trainor & Associates
537 Houston Street
Monterey, CA 93940
831-655-1414
bernard@bernardtrainor.com
www.bernardtrainor.com

Shirley Alexander Watts
sawattsdesign
1000 Park Street
Alameda, CA 94501
510-521-5223
sawattscdf@gmail.com
www.sawattsdesign.com

Susan Welti and Paige Keck
Foras Studio LLC
Brooklyn, New York
info@foras-studio.com
www.foras-studio.com

Mark Word
Mark Word Design
P.O. Box 41718
Austin, Texas 78704
512-440-0013
designoffice@markworddesign.com
www.markworddesign.com

Featured Organizations

Chicago Honey Co-op
Michael S. Thompson
Chicago, Illinois
www.chicagohoneycoop.com

City Farm / Resource Center
Chicago, Illinois
cityfarm@resourcecenterchicago.org
www.resourcecenterchicago.org

Eagle Street Rooftop Farm
Annie Novak
Brooklyn, New York
http://rooftopfarms.org/
www.GrowingChefs.org

Gary Comer Youth Center
7200 South Ingleside Avenue
Chicago, IL 60619
773-358-4100
www.gcyhome.org

Growing Gardens
2003 NE 42nd Avenue, #3
Portland, OR 97213
503-284-8420
www.growing-gardens.org

Growing Power
Erika Allen
2215 W. North Avenue
Chicago, IL 60647
773-486-6005
www.growingpower.org

Silver Lake Farms
Tara Kolla
Los Angeles, California
323-644-3700
info@silverlakefarms.com
www.silverlakefarms.com

Urban Farm Store
Robert Litt
2100 SE Belmont Street
Portland, OR 97214
503-234-7733
info@urbanfarmstore.com
www.urbanfarmstore.com

Acknowledgments

I GIVE SPECIAL THANKS to all the designers and makers of the beautiful gardens who opened their homes to me, often on short notice and at odd hours. I also very much appreciate the hospitable friends who let me stay with them while I traveled around to photograph this book on a tight budget: Barbara Farmer, Susan Burke, Clay Hunn, Alta Tingle, and Susan Oppie. It couldn't have happened otherwise. I relied heavily on several astute manuscript readers: Barbara Farmer, Betsy Beckmann, Chad Jacobs, Clay Hunn, and Melissa Ozawa. Many thanks to photographer Dana Gallagher, who taught me to how to look at the light. To my agent, Carla Glasser, who sealed the deal during very uncertain economic times. To my editor, Pam Krauss, who doesn't sugarcoat her feedback but is usually right. To the book's designer, Kara Plikaitis, for her collaborative spirit. Thank you to my mother for introducing me to Dr. D. G. Hessayon and for the Abilene Public Library for introducing me to the Lorax. Most of all, thank you to the two most important people in my life: my father who taught me to value books and respect growing things during the first two decades of my life, and my partner, Chad Jacobs, who taught me to love life over these last 25 years.